Simply Mediterranean

Recipes for a Good Life

Simply Mediterranean

The whole Mediterranean—the sculptures, the palms, the gold beads, the bearded heroes, the wine, the ideas, the ships, the moonlight, the winged gorgons, the bronze men, the philosophers—all of it seems to rise in the sour, pungent taste of these black olives between the teeth. A taste older than meat, older than wine. A taste as old as cold water.

– Lawrence Durrell, *Prospero's Cell*

This book is dedicated to all who have contributed their time, effort, expertise, and support in our journey to bring responsibly produced, authentic specialty foods to the U.S. consumer. From the field to the fork, our small but strong community has done so much to carry on the culinary traditions and heritage of the Mediterranean.

Thank you.

Simply Mediterranean
(Recipes for a Good Life)
©2017 by FOODMatch, Inc.

Written by Phil Meldrum
with Brandon Gross & Brett Greenberg
Foreword by Michael Psilakis ©2017
Design by Reid Hamilton
Photographs ©2017 FOODMatch, Inc.
(unless noted below)
iStock.com contributors: zeljkosantrac (pg. 18), istetiana (pg. 19), Spiderstock (pg. 42), photooiasson (pg. 43), mihailomilovanovic (pg. 78), Tramont_ana (pg. 93), supermimicry (pg. 116), mediaphotos (pg. 117), deyangeorgiev (pg. 144), nimis69 (pg. 145), sandsun (pg. 163), ilbusca (pg. 186), Kelly Cline (pg. 187), AlexRaths (pg. 191, 192), Bepsimage (pg. 201).

Published by FOODMatch, Inc.
575 8th Avenue, Floor 23
New York, NY 10018
www.foodmatch.com

ISBN-13 #: 978-0-9981147-0-5
Production & Design by FOODMatch, Inc.
Printed in China
First Edition 2017

Table of Contents

Foreword
Food Memories

As with all first-generation children, I learned quickly that the picture snapped in my parents' mind, as they left their country for a brighter future in a foreign land, would serve as a vacuum of customs, traditions, morals, religion, and of course food in which my siblings and I were raised. For better or worse, I grew up immersed in that picture of Greece, almost recklessly, as I straddled the two worlds of Greeks and non-Greeks. I quickly began to realize that the two were not the same, and nothing defined that more than the food that we ate. The meals my mother cooked daily were guarded by her love of tradition. They contained stories, memories, and life lessons. The meals reflected a culture that saw food as a mechanism to gather, either from simple socializations to grand celebrations or to the mourning of a loved one. Food was not a means of living; it was a way of living. Dinner was not a meal as much as it was an opportunity for my mother to gather her family at a table and provide them with the gift of food.

I remember watching her prepare those meals and wondering why she was always the last one to sit down at the table, at the seat closest to the kitchen, caring more about what or how much others ate rather than what she ate. I realized that the joy of the meals she cooked was having us there, together, as a family, sharing our thoughts, problems, and joys. She taught me the beauty of the gift of food. It was through her hands that I saw love become a meal.

My father, on the other hand, never lifted a hand in the kitchen. I doubt he even knew where a pot could be found. From him, I learned that food did not come form a store, on a Styrofoam plate wrapped in plastic. He taught me what it was like to prepare a garden and cultivate its jewels, how to hunt or fish for an animal, and how to take the seeds from the late harvest vegetables and save them for next year's crop. He would always remind me of his childhood in the mountains of Crete, where a day of work promised food to eat, not from the earning it paid but rather from the vegetable or animal for which you cared. He deeply respected these things. Nature was a means of surviving, a way of life, and somehow a teacher of all things. I just had to listen.

As a chef who never went to culinary school, never apprenticed in another's kitchen, and never traveled enough to be influenced by other cultures, my style of food emerged from these memories. I remember the simple salad of tomato, pulled off the vine, served with sliced onion, and drizzled with red wine vinegar, olive oil, and oregano, that we hung upside down in the garage to dry; plates were heaped with olives, cheese, roasted and preserved vegetables; and warm bread taken right from the oven would be saturated with unfiltered olive oil that was flavored with fruit and yet finished with sharp acidity and fiery bite. For years, I imagined how I could use these ingredients to take someone on a journey to my mother's table or my father's garden.

As you skim through this book and become inspired by the extraordinary pictures, recipes, and stories that you will find on its pages, I hope you use them as my parents once did with the simple picture of life that they took with them when they left Greece. Use them to give the gift of food to your family and friends; use them as a vehicle to gather as often as you can; use them to compose an infinite amount of memorable meals; but most important, use them to create memories that will last a lifetime and beyond.

– Michael Psilakis, Chef/owner, Kefi, FISHTAG, MP Taverna

The annual olive
harvest in Greece

Introduction
The Gift of the Olive

So much of Mediterranean culture can be traced back to the olive, a simple fruit that is not only the culinary foundation of antiquity, but has also become a symbol of peace and prosperity.

Legend has it that Zeus held a contest between Athena and Poseidon to see who could produce the most valuable gift to mankind. The winner would have a new city named after them. With great force, Poseidon threw his trident against the rock of the Acropolis. A spring shot forth but the water was salty. Then Athena, kneeling, put her staff into the ground and an olive tree sprang up, laden with fruit. Zeus ruled that the olive tree was the most valuable gift and the new city was named Athens in honor of Athena. To this day, a lone olive tree sits on top of the Acropolis to symbolize Athena's gift.

Nature confirms that the olive is truly a gift to mankind. Unlike many other fruit trees, the olive propagates through its roots. Its fruit, the olive, has no real biological value to the tree. Yet, for thousands of years, the olive has been a source of sustenance for mankind.

On an Island in Greece

More than twenty years ago, my wife Chantal and I were wandering through an ancient, breathtaking olive grove on a Greek island in the Ionian Sea. Somehow, while exploring the craggy slope, we managed to lose our sense of direction. I knew we weren't hopelessly lost, so when we paused beneath the rustling, silvery-green canopy of a particularly majestic tree, it was not so much to get our bearings as to rest a bit and let the splendor we were experiencing soak in. The legions of gnarled trees around us glowed as if gilded in the waning afternoon sun. Our idyllic days on the island, the warm golden light, and the waves of the cicada chorus that ebbed and flowed around us in the centuries-old olive trees all stirred our hearts. The moment was sublime.

Our thoughts turned to the antiquity of the trees, some of which locals had told us were planted by the Venetians. We marveled at what human folly those trees may have witnessed over the centuries. So much has changed since they first took root, yet so much of what we had experienced on that trip remained unchanged through the ages. Like the grove, the local customs and traditions that we took such delight in were seemingly eternal.

We were fortunate to have been able to immerse ourselves in the wonderful lifestyle of the island, one that often extends well beyond the boundaries of the island to the entire Mediterranean. This lifestyle values traditions, community, family, and time, and its purest expression is in the sharing of unhurried, beautiful, healthful meals, simply prepared with local ingredients. At those tables, food is love.

We found our way back up the hills to our host's home overlooking the sea. At that moment, I became determined to find a way to share and recreate a true Mediterranean experience for others back home. What better way than to introduce the wonderful regional specialties of the Mediterranean to the American table? Using simple Mediterranean-style ingredients and recipes on the following pages, we can all enjoy the culinary and cultural heritage of the Mediterranean and bring some of that lifestyle into our own lives.

Cheers!

– Phil Meldrum

Anna's Taverna

In a tiny village outside Sparta is Anna's, a small taverna named after its owner, founder, cook, host, server, dishwasher, and cashier. Like so many of the tavernas scattered throughout the villages and islands of Greece, Anna's is a favorite gathering spot where locals meet daily to chat over simple meals of fresh, local ingredients.

Anna greets each of her guests with a warm smile and heart-melting hug before ushering them to one of the rough-hewn communal tables that wobble endearingly on the well-worn terracotta floor. She pours her guests a glass of local wine, puts down a cruet of freshly pressed olive oil and board of bread, hot from the oven (none of which was ordered). Then, before anyone can utter "Efcharisto" (thank you), Anna rushes back into the kitchen to prepare lunch.

While patrons chat in Anna's cheerful dining room, a tantalizing array of sensual temptations waft from the kitchen: the sizzle of the wood-fired grill as Anna deftly turns a lamb chop liberally seasoned with salt pepper and wild oregano; the "opo" of the cork from yet another bottle of wine; the heady arrival of charred octopus in all its smoky, buttery splendor; and the steady stream of brightly hued platters filled with wilted "horta" (wild greens), julienned cabbage and carrots, smoky grilled peppers, and tomato-cucumber-olive salad with feta and capers, each brightened with plenty of local olive oil and lemon. All the while, the locals continue to arrive, laughing, smiling, and launching into stories of the day.

There is a sense of magic at Anna's Taverna, where meals are much more than sitting and eating well. Patrons are not just guests, they are family and friends, or nearly so, and lunches at Anna's are fluid, neighborly affairs that often spill outdoors to the sun-bleached tables in the village square overlooking the surrounding hills. This is a way of life that values simplicity, time, and community: children dart merrily in and out of always-open doorways, drying clothes flutter from windows, and neighborhood dogs cozy up indiscriminately at diners' feet. And more often than not, musicians, always eager to play for even the smallest of crowds, approach from around the corner.

On cue, Anna slips inside and reappears with coffee, pastries, and ouzo. She lingers in the background, standing beneath the Greek flag that hangs over the taverna door. She quietly observes the community, one that she has had a hand in building and nurturing. As friends dance and sing, Anna smiles so widely that her eyes seem to close, at one with the collective happiness around her. When the villagers finally decide to call it a night, there is a sense of joy and relief all around. Everything will begin anew tomorrow.

Anna (left) and
her mother

Olive producers in
Kefalas Village, just
outside of Sparta

It Takes a Village

The story of how a small farming community in Greece saved their land and preserved a centuries-old culinary heritage.

Kefalas Village is a tiny hamlet of dusty white roads, thyme-covered fields, craggy rock outcroppings, and a few hundred hardy souls. Located in the mountainous foothills just outside of ancient Sparta, the village's stone fences cleave tenaciously to the steep, rocky hillside as they twist their way upward through the reluctant but fertile land, crisscrossing through rugged groves of magnificent olive trees. It is a lovely place that owes much of its beauty to the locale. Its residents also owe their livelihood to the land. As with so many of the small villages throughout Greece, the land is the main provider of jobs and income for locals, many of whom are descended from a long lineage of skilled farmers and craftsmen. In Kefalas, work, life, livelihood, and play are centered exclusively on olive cultivation.

So, imagine the fear that struck this community when, in the summer of 2007, a widespread wildfire threatened not only the families and their homes, but also the acres upon acres of olive trees that provided the villagers with their sole source of income. Fortuitously, after a previous devastating wildfire in 1998, the growers in Kefalas Village made the decision to convert their farm vehicles into hybrid firetrucks, and collectively they outfitted their motley assortment of tractors with pumps that could be instantly fitted with water hoses. As the wildfire of 2007 approached the village, the men readied their tractors, while the women and children stood guard at the crest of the highest hill in the town. This community was prepared to fight for what they held most dear; the Kalamata olive.

The community effort was a success. After the villagers created a dry perimeter of land around the village to act as a barrier, they positioned their tractors to battle the approaching fire. The pumps and hoses on the tractors were strong enough to squelch the flames and divert the fires from their land.

The story of how Kefalas Village was spared by the wildfire of 2007 has become legend, to be shared with each new generation as a lesson in the true meaning of community, in particular the power of collective resourcefulness, teamwork, and pride of place. Today, the sweeping views from the church of thousands of olive trees is more breathtaking than ever, perhaps because we know how close all of it came to being stolen away.

1.

Dress It Up

Vinaigrettes, Sauces & Spreads

Our go-to dressings, sauces, and spreads weave together many classic Mediterranean ingredients like olives, lemons, tomatoes, and capers. Drizzle 'em, slather 'em, or spoon 'em onto your favorite, everyday menu ingredients and marvel at the unexpected flair and excitement they add to your crisp salad greens, simple pieces of grilled meat, and bowls of al dente pasta. Think of these recipes as inspirations for imparting a signature flourish to your own dishes!

Everyday Vinaigrette

{ makes about ⅓ cup, enough for a salad for 4 }

This recipe makes enough vinaigrette to dress 4 to 6 cups of salad greens. We make the dressing right in the salad bowl, then pile chilled lettuce leaves on top. Take the salad to the table and toss it just before you are ready to serve it. No up and down and back and forth to the kitchen, and the lettuce stays crisp and crunchy. This is a trick every hostess should know. This is our go-to vinaigrette.

½–1 clove garlic, peeled and minced
1 teaspoon Dijon mustard
Salt
Freshly ground black pepper
1 tablespoon red wine vinegar or fresh lemon juice
3–4 tablespoons extra-virgin olive oil

Put the garlic, mustard, a pinch of salt, and some pepper into a salad bowl and stir together with a wooden spoon. Stir in the vinegar. Add the olive oil, stirring it in. Adjust the seasonings.

SIMPLE TIP
Like your vinaigrettes a little sweet? Try adding a teaspoon of honey. Like it spicy? Add a few dashes of hot sauce.

Anchovy Vinaigrette

{ makes about ⅓ cup, enough for a salad for 4 }

The lovely anchovy is often misunderstood, it has the reputation of tasting a little too "fishy". But anchovies can improve the flavor of all sorts of foods without adding any overt fishiness. We love the way they add salt, depth of flavor, and even a little *umami* to foods. In this vinaigrette the anchovies soften the acid of the vinegar or lemon juice. When you are mincing them, add a little salt for grit, then mince and mash them with the flat side of a knife.

6–8 anchovy fillets, minced and mashed
1 clove garlic, peeled and minced
Salt
Freshly ground black pepper
1 tablespoon red or white wine vinegar or fresh lemon juice
4 tablespoons extra-virgin olive oil

Put the anchovies, garlic, a pinch of salt (not too much as the anchovies are salty), and some pepper into a small bowl and mix together with a spoon. Stir in the vinegar. Add the olive oil, stirring it in. Adjust the seasonings.

SIMPLE TIP
Add a bit of freshly grated Parmesan and you're on your way to a simplified version of the classic Caesar dressing.

Green Olive Vinaigrette

{ makes about ½ cup, enough for a salad for 4–6 }

Italian Castelvetrano or Cerignola olives, with their vibrant green and buttery-tasting flesh, are delicious in this vinaigrette, though any variety of pitted green olive can be used. Their vibrant color comes from being picked before they fully ripen to a dark purplish black. Sometimes we use anchovy-stuffed Manzanilla olives for this vinaigrette.

¼ cup pitted green olives, chopped
1 small clove garlic, peeled and minced
1 tablespoon white wine vinegar or fresh lemon juice
Pinch of crushed red pepper flakes
Salt
Freshly ground black pepper
4 tablespoons extra-virgin olive oil

Put the olives, garlic, vinegar, red pepper flakes, a pinch of salt, and some pepper into a small bowl and stir together. Add the olive oil, stirring it in. Adjust the seasonings.

Black Olive Spread Vinaigrette

{ makes about ½ cup, enough for a salad for 4–6 }

The great thing about olive spread is that all the work is done for you—no pitting or chopping— and it mixes smoothly and easily into vinaigrette. It's perfect for green salads or sliced tomatoes, and delicious spooned onto grilled salmon or other seafood. We stir it into cooked white beans, then add chopped scallions or sautéed shallots. We're sure you'll think up favorites of your own.

¼ cup kalamata olive spread or finely chopped, pitted black olives
2–3 tablespoons finely chopped fresh parsley leaves
1 small clove garlic, peeled and minced
1 tablespoon red wine vinegar
4–6 tablespoons extra-virgin olive oil
Salt
Freshly ground black pepper

Put the olive spread, parsley, garlic, vinegar, and olive oil into a medium bowl and stir together. Season with salt and pepper. This vinaigrette keeps in the refrigerator, covered, for up to 1 week.

Preserved Lemon Vinaigrette

{ makes about ½ cup, enough for a salad for 4–6 }

This bright vinaigrette is a breeze to make. Super on salads, try spooning it over roast chicken or fish at room temperature.

2 tablespoons fresh lemon juice
1 tablespoon preserved lemon spread
⅓ cup extra-virgin olive oil
Salt
Freshly ground black pepper

Put the lemon juice and preserved lemon spread into a small bowl. Stir in the olive oil. Season to taste with a little salt and pepper.

Harissa Vinaigrette

{ makes about ⅔ cup, enough for a salad for 6 }

Harissa is a garlicky chile paste used in cooking across North Africa in Morrocco, Algeria, and Tunisia. Ground, roasted red chiles are mixed with spices such as coriander seeds, saffron, and caraway along with garlic and olive oil. The recipe varies from place to place and household to household. We love the heat and warm flavor it adds to this vinaigrette.

1 clove garlic, peeled and minced
Pinch of fennel seeds, chopped
Pinch of cumin seeds, chopped
Salt
Freshly ground black pepper
2 tablespoons harissa paste
2 tablespoons red wine vinegar or fresh lemon juice
6 tablespoons extra-virgin olive oil

Put the garlic, fennel, cumin, a good pinch of salt, and some pepper into a small bowl. Stir in the harissa and vinegar. Add the olive oil, stirring it in. Adjust the seasonings.

Caper-Cornichon Mayonnaise

{ makes about 1¼ cups }

This is our version of tartar sauce and the perfect complement for any deep-fried food—fish, shoe-string potatoes, pickles, and on and on. Cornichons and capers are its distinguishing flavors. Cornichons are pickled French gherkin cucumbers, small in size but big in crunch and tart flavor. Capers (the edible flower buds of the *Capparis* shrub) are found in countries surrounding the Mediterranean. They are hand-picked, then preserved in salt or in brine. Both of these ingredients add bright notes to this creamy, tangy sauce.

Stir together 1 cup mayonnaise, 8 chopped cornichons, 1 tablespoon capers plus 1 teaspoon of the pickling brine, 2 tablespoons fresh lemon juice, and 4 finely chopped sprigs each fresh parsley, dill, and tarragon in a medium bowl. Season with salt and freshly ground black pepper. The mayonnaise keeps in the refrigerator, covered, for up to 1 week.

SIMPLE TIP
Kids will love this recipe mixed with equal parts ketchup. It's a Mediterranean take on "special sauce" that's perfect for burgers.

Roasted Tomato Vinaigrette

{ makes about ½ cup, enough for a salad for 4–6 }

We slow-roast tomatoes with extra-virgin olive oil, garlic, spices, and a splash of vinegar to bring a sweet, rich flavor to this mellow vinaigrette. It's a way to get a taste of summer even in the middle of winter.

¼ cup roasted tomatoes, finely chopped
1 small clove garlic, peeled and minced
1 tablespoon chopped fresh parsley leaves
Salt
Freshly ground black pepper
1 tablespoon red wine vinegar or fresh lemon juice
4–5 tablespoons extra-virgin olive oil

Put the roasted tomatoes, garlic, parsley, a pinch of salt, and some pepper into a small bowl and stir together. Stir in the vinegar. Add the olive oil, stirring it in. Adjust the seasonings.

SIMPLE TIP
At your next party, serve this vinaigrette drizzled over fresh mozzarella.

Green Olive Mayonnaise

{ makes about 2¼ cups }

If you've a mind to, you can make your own mayonnaise from scratch, but we usually buy a good prepared mayonnaise—it's easier, quicker, and still very good. We make this green olive mayo to spread on sandwiches, spoon on cold poached chicken or grilled fish. Try mixing it with canned tuna for a twist on tuna salad.

1 cup mayonnaise
1 cup pitted citrus-stuffed olives or other pitted green olives, finely chopped
1 cup fresh parsley leaves, finely chopped
1 small shallot, peeled and minced
Rind of ½ preserved lemon, minced
Freshly ground black pepper

Stir together the mayonnaise, olives, parsley, shallots, and lemon rind in a medium bowl. Season to taste with pepper. The mayonnaise keeps in the refrigerator, covered, for up to 1 week.

Lemon-Anchovy Mayonnaise

{ makes about 1¼ cups }

Preserved lemon rind is a great way to add a complex salty flavor to food. Spread this mayonnaise on sliced tomatoes, boiled potatoes, and poached fish. Use it to make chicken or tuna salad. We even serve it with spicy Buffalo chicken wings for a sophisticated twist.

1 cup mayonnaise
2 tablespoons preserved lemon spread
8 anchovy fillets, minced
Pinch of crushed red pepper flakes

Stir together the mayonnaise, preserved lemon spread, anchovies, and red pepper flakes in a medium bowl. The mayonnaise keeps in the refrigerator, covered, for up to 1 week.

SIMPLE TIP
A pinch of Old Bay Seasoning makes this the perfect dip for crab cakes or shrimp cocktail.

Simply Mediterranean

Salsa Verde

{ makes 2 cups }

Though many countries have their version of this sauce, the best known is from Italy. The Italians traditionally serve this "green sauce" with boiled meats. But its deep green, piquant flavor complements everything from fish to steamed vegetables. We like to stir a spoonful into soups, vinaigrettes, beans, and stews. Substitute basil for a more Italian flavor.

2 cups fresh parsley leaves, chopped
½ cup pitted Castelvetrano or other green olives, chopped
4 scallions, trimmed and chopped
4 sprigs tarragon, chopped
3 anchovy fillets, chopped
1 clove garlic, peeled and minced
1 tablespoon capers
2 tablespoons white wine vinegar or fresh lemon juice
1 cup extra-virgin olive oil
Salt
Freshly ground black pepper

Put the parsley, olives, scallions, tarragon, anchovies, garlic, capers, vinegar, and olive oil into a medium bowl and stir well. Season with salt and pepper. Adjust the flavors with a little more vinegar if you want a brighter, sharper flavored sauce, or with more olive oil if you want it milder.

Tomato Sauce for Pasta & Pizza

{ makes about 2 cups }

This classic all-purpose tomato sauce is simple and quick to make. It relies on the best canned tomatoes (we use Italian San Marzano) and really good extra-virgin olive oil. It is the all-purpose sauce that we use for spaghetti, lasagne, and pizza. At this point we all know it by heart—we hope you will too.

One 28-ounce can crushed tomatoes
1 onion, peeled and halved lengthwise
1 clove garlic, peeled and crushed
1 sprig fresh basil
½ cup extra-virgin olive oil
Salt
Freshly ground black pepper

Pour the tomatoes into a heavy medium pot. Rinse the can with ½ cup water and add it to the pot. Add the onions, garlic, basil, and olive oil. Season with salt and pepper.

Simmer over medium-low heat, stirring occasionally, until the onions are soft and the sauce thickens, about 30 minutes. Adjust the seasonings and add a little more olive oil if you want to reduce the acidic flavor of the sauce. Remove and discard the onions and basil before using.

Tomato & Olive Sauce

{ makes about 3 cups }

Follow the above recipe, adding 1 cup thickly sliced, pitted, green Cerignola olives and 2 pinches of crushed red pepper flakes to the pot.

2.

Pairings

Curated by Chef Michael Psilakis

As a child, I remember bowls of olives sitting on the kitchen table along with some feta cheese and slices of crusty, rustic bread.

It was almost impossible to go from one room to the next without quickly tossing a few in your mouth. As an adult, that same combination paired with a glass of wine, a few slices of fatty salami, barrel-aged feta, and some preserved vegetables became a meal. Each element adds another layer to the overall experience.

"THAT FIVE-SECOND EXPERIENCE…"

As a chef, I'm challenged on a daily basis to create a bite of food that not only resonates on the palate but has a spectrum of taste that evolves from beginning, middle, and end. To a chef, food is articulated in that five-second experience. A simple way to create that experience is to use ingredients that already possess deep, layered flavor profiles as a garnish or condiment to evolve the one-dimensional palate experience. In the Mediterranean, no single item does that more than the olive.

PAIRING

Gone are the days of canned black olives being a go-to household staple. The good news is that there are so many different olive varietals being sold at local markets. The challenge is making sense of them all and figuring out what varietal will taste best with your favorite cheeses.

To me, the joy of eating olives is all about how the flavor resonates with your palate. There is no need to get technical, but if you want a little guidance, the curing style of an olive (the process that turns an olive from bitter and inedible to sweet and delicious) plays a big part in determining how it tastes and what it pairs with.

Here are some pairings to get you started as you begin your own journey.

– Chef Michael Psilakis

Olive Curing Style:
Brine Cured, Unfermented Green

Olive Varietals: Lucque, Picholine, Castelvetrano

Cheese Pairings: Chèvre, Comté, Brie, Burrata, Buffalo Mozzarella, Triple-crème, Fromager d'Affinois

Wine & Beer Parings: Sauvignon Blanc, Champagne and session beers (mild, 3-4% ABV)

Mild (1) to Strong (5): 1 of 5

Chef's Notes: These are my go-to olives for delicate proteins such as smoked salmon, prawns, and chicken. Their flavor is wonderfully mild, fresh, and buttery. I particularly enjoy their crisp and slightly firm texture.

Lucques, Castelvetrano,
Bucheron, Comté,
Fromage d'Affinois,
salumi, sessions beer,
Champagne, baguette.

Ripe black Greek olives, black Cerignola, Nebbiolo, Altbier, saucisson sec, Genoa salami, fresh ricotta, Camembert, le Chevrot and freshly baked bread.

Olive Curing Style:
Brine Cured, Oxidized Black

Olive Varietals: Black Cerignola, Greek "Ripe" Black

Cheese Pairings: Fresh Mozzarella, Ricotta, Fontina, aged goat's milk (firm or
                           soft), Camembert

Wine & Beer Parings: Pinot Noir, Nebbiolo, Loire Valley Cabernet Franc, Altbier

Mild (1) to Strong (5):   2 of 5

Chef's Notes: Today there are far better artisanal versions of oxidized
                           black olives than the ones from tin cans you're likely used
                           to from childhood! Oxidized black olives are defined by a
                           mild flavor profile with subtle hints of fruit. In my opinion,
                           they are best when used as an accent to a mild cheese or a
                           composed plate of food (think tacos, nachos, chili, etc.).

Olive Curing Style:
Brine Cured, Fermented Green

Olive Varietals: Halkidiki (Mt. Athos), Green Cerignola, Green Beldi, Ascolana, Sevillano, Cassées des Baux, Manzanilla

Cheese Pairings: Taleggio, aged Provolone, clothbound Cheddar, aged Gouda, Iberico, and Manchego

Wine & Beer Parings: Sancerre, Grüner, Vermentino, unfiltered wheat beer

Mild (1) to Strong (5):   3 of 5

Chef's Notes: Brine-cured and fermented green olives have nutty, herbal undertones with a long, tangy finish. These olives have great depth of flavor, so you can turn up the volume with pairings. For antipasti, I like to serve these olives with thin slices of prosciutto di Parma, marinated artichokes, and Marcona almonds.

Green Beldi, Halkidiki "Mt. Athos,"
Sevillano, aged gouda, Taleggio,
clothbound cheddar, Manchego,
prosciutto, Grüner.

Kalamata,
Alfonso, Gaeta,
Niçoise, Feta,
Blue d'Auvergne,
Parmigiano-
Reggiano, sweet
soppressata,
Pilsner, Cabernet
Sauvignon.

Olive Curing Style:
Brine Cured, Fermented Mature (Purple/Black)

Olive Varietals:	Kalamata, Niçoise, Alfonso, Arbequina, Amfissa (Mt. Pelion), Gordal, Nafplion, Gaeta
Cheese Pairings:	Greek Feta, Parmigiano-Reggiano, Pecorino, Bleu d'Auvergne
Wine & Beer Parings:	Cabernet Sauvignon, Merlot, Côtes du Rhône, Sangiovese, Pilsner
Mild (1) to Strong (5):	4 of 5
Chef's Notes:	Kings of the olive world, these beauties are harvested at the end of the season and cure for 4-6 months. This results in strong flavor notes of smoke and red wine. With regard to food and beverage pairings, these olives are flavorful enough to pair with aged beef, game birds, lamb, and aged or stinky cheeses.

Olive Curing Style:
Dry Cured (Oil or Salt Cured)

Olive Varietals: Beldi, Thassos, Nyon

Cheese Pairings: Cave-aged Gruyère, Stilton, Gorgonzola

Wine & Beer Parings: Ice cold lager, Malbec, Cabernet

Mild (1) to Strong (5):   5 of 5

Chef's Notes: These olives have a highly concentrated, fruit-
                            forward flavor with intense undertones of licorice,
                            stone fruit, and tobacco. At the restaurant, we often
                            dice them as small as possible and use them as we
                            would normally use sea salt to finish a dish. I often
                            refer to dry cured olives as hurdles in a race: you
                            know they are coming but you still have to prepare
                            yourself each time you reach one. Their assertive
                            nature lends them to stinky and blue-veined cheeses
                            and hearty braises of beef or lamb.

Black Beldi, Thassos,
Gorgonzola, Stilton,
Gruyère, pork salami,
Malbec, lager

3.

Salads & Sides

Mediterranean cooking is all about creating satisfying flavors from simple, wholesome ingredients. Our flavorful side dishes, built on the foundations of the Mediterranean diet, are lean, green – and loaded with protein, fiber, and heart-friendly olive oil. They're not only delicious and easy to prepare, they're healthy for you, too. Enjoy them as sides or as a main course; either way, they just might steal the show.

Simply Mediterranean

Sliced Tomatoes with Green Olive Vinaigrette

{ serves 4 }

Ripe summer tomatoes are ideal for this salad. However, we find the flavorful meatiness of the olive vinaigrette makes even less than perfect tomatoes sing.

Core and slice a combination of tomatoes: 2 large, 3 medium, and 12 small or cherry size (or any comparable quantity). Vary the variety and color and use your favorites. Arrange them on 4 salad plates. Spoon 1 cup Green Olive Vinaigrette (page 27) over the tomatoes. Season with salt and freshly ground black pepper.

Hearts of Palm, Orange, & Belgian Endive Salad

{ serves 2 }

Although this juicy salad can be prepared with tender, unseasoned hearts of palm, we prefer the way the fresh and crisp pickled ones complement the sweetness of the orange segments. If you can, look for marinated (bread and butter or sweet picante) hearts of palm.

½ clove garlic, peeled and minced
½ teaspoon Dijon mustard
Salt
Freshly ground black pepper
1 teaspoon white wine vinegar
3–4 tablespoons extra-virgin olive oil
1 navel orange
½–⅓ cup pickled hearts of palm, including pickled jalapeño slices
2 heads Belgian endive, leaves separated and halved lengthwise

SIMPLE TIP
Pickled hearts of palm are a great substitute for traditional cucumber pickles in a Cuban sandwich.

Put the garlic, mustard, a pinch of salt, and some pepper into a medium bowl and stir together with a wooden spoon. Stir in the vinegar. Add the olive oil, stirring it in. Adjust the seasonings. Set aside.

Slice off the ends of the orange. Set the orange on one end and slice off the rind and white pith, exposing the flesh. Working over the bowl of vinaigrette to catch any juice, slice between each fruit segment, cutting it away from the membrane and letting the segments and juice fall into the bowl. Squeeze any juice from the spent fruit into the bowl. Add the hearts of palm and jalapeño slices and Belgian endive to the bowl and toss well.

Divide the salad between two plates. Serve each salad with a piece of buttered bread topped with slices of smoked salmon and garnished with capers and chopped fresh chives, if you like.

Marinated Beet & Radicchio Salad

{ serves 4 }

This salad, bejeweled with garnet-like pieces of marinated beets, is a perennial favorite served on its own or with roasted or grilled meats or fish.

2–3 inner stalks of celery, chopped
⅔ cup Anchovy Vinaigrette (page 24)
1 head radicchio, leaves separated and torn in half or thirds
¼ red onion, peeled and thinly sliced
1 cup marinated beets, cut into large dice
½ cup celery leaves

Toss the celery and half the vinaigrette in a large bowl. Just before serving the salad, add the radicchio and onions and toss well, adding more vinaigrette according to taste. Transfer the salad to a serving platter. Scatter the beets on top and garnish with celery leaves.

Carrot, Currant, Caper & Parsley Salad

{ serves 2 }

We like to make this crunchy Middle Eastern-inspired salad ahead of time. Then, just before we're ready to eat, we add a dollop of cool yogurt and a drizzle of honey.

¼ cup dried currants
⅓ cup Harissa Vinaigrette (page 28)
2–3 carrots, peeled and cut into short, thin strips or grated (about 2 cups)
2 tablespoons capers, drained
1 cup tightly packed parsley leaves, chopped
Salt
Freshly ground black pepper
½ cup plain yogurt
2 tablespoons honey

Toss the currants in the vinaigrette in a medium bowl and set aside to macerate for 20–30 minutes. Add the carrots, capers, and parsley to the bowl and toss well. Season with a little salt and pepper. The salad is ready to serve, but can be stored in the refrigerator, covered, for up to 2 days. Serve the carrot salad as is, or divide it between two bowls and top with a dollop of yogurt and a drizzle of honey.

Shrimp Salad with Hearts of Palm

{ serves 4 }

Preserved lemon spread, the smooth paste made from preserved lemon rinds, is full of salty, deep lemon flavor. If the spread is not available but preserved lemons are, make your own paste. Barring that, a good squeeze of fresh lemon juice will do the trick of brightening this shrimp salad.

¼ cup mayonnaise
1 tablespoon preserved lemon spread
2 anchovy fillets, minced
1 tablespoon fresh lemon juice
24 cooked medium shrimp, peeled, deveined, and chilled
1 head bibb lettuce, leaves separated
12 slices marinated hearts of palm, cut into strips
1 small jalapeño, stemmed, seeded, and finely diced

Mix the mayonnaise, preserved lemon spread, anchovies, and lemon juice together in a medium bowl until smooth. Add the shrimp and toss until they are evenly coated. Chill until ready to serve. Divide the lettuce leaves between four salad plates. Arrange 6 shrimp on top of the lettuce on each plate. Garnish each plate with some of the hearts of palm and the jalapeño.

Marinated Gigandes Beans with Tuna

{ serves 2 }

A plate of tender beans, like these huge, marinated gigandes, and tuna packed in olive oil make a quick and satisfying lunch. Sometimes, we'll dress them up a little and serve this simple salad with peppery arugula and hard-boiled eggs. Marinated gigandes beans can be found at the olive and antipasti bar of most grocery stores.

Divide 2 cups marinated gigandes beans between two plates. Place 2–3 ounces tuna packed in olive oil and drained, on top of the beans. Squeeze the juice of half a lemon over the tuna and beans. Drizzle with some extra-virgin olive oil. Season with a little salt and freshly ground black pepper. Garnish the salads with some fresh thyme and a wedge of lemon.

Tabbouleh with Roasted Tomatoes

{ serves 4 }

We've taken liberties with this Middle Eastern bulgur-flecked herb salad and substituted roasted tomatoes for raw. They give it a more robust flavor, though the fresh parsley and mint are really the outstanding heroes.

1 cup whole-grain red bulgur
4 cups parsley leaves, finely chopped
1 bunch scallions, trimmed and finely chopped
1 cup mint leaves, finely chopped
½ cup roasted tomatoes, finely chopped
Juice of 2 lemons
3 tablespoons extra-virgin olive oil
Salt
Freshly ground black pepper

Put the bulgur and 1 cup boiling water into a large bowl. Let sit until the bulgur swells and has absorbed all the water, about 1 hour. Fluff the bulgur with a fork.

Add the parsley, scallions, mint, and roasted tomatoes to the bowl and toss well. Season with the lemon juice, olive oil, salt, and pepper to taste. Serve at room temperature.

Roasted Red Peppers with Currants & Capers

{ serves 4–8 }

We serve this meaty, sweet pepper salad with meze or along with other big flavors, like smoky grilled lamb, chicken, or fish. Roast your own peppers or use the prized fire-roasted Florina peppers from Greece.

½ cup extra-virgin olive oil
2 tablespoons dried currants
2 tablespoons capers, drained
Juice of 1 lemon
8 roasted sweet peppers
1 small handful fresh mint leaves
Salt
Freshly ground black pepper

Put the olive oil, currants, capers, and lemon juice into a deep serving dish. Set aside and let the currants marinate and soften for 30 minutes.

Nestle the roasted peppers into the dish with the currants. Add the mint, season with salt and pepper, and turn the peppers until they are well coated. Let them marinate for an hour or so before serving.

SIMPLE TIP
Serve with a bottle of Rioja, aged Manchego, and some crusty bread.

Torchetti with Olives, Capers & Lemon

{ serves 2–4 }

Any green olive will do for this green sauce, but we particularly like using Sicilian Castelvetrano. They are the prettiest bright green, meaty, and sweet.

½ cup green olives, pitted and coarsely chopped
1 cup parsley leaves, finely chopped
1 tablespoon capers, drained and chopped
4 cloves pickled garlic, minced
4 anchovy fillets, minced
1–2 teaspoons finely chopped preserved lemon rind or 1 teaspoon finely grated lemon zest
1–2 pinches of crushed red pepper flakes
Juice of ½–1 lemon
¼ cup extra-virgin olive oil
Salt
Freshly ground black pepper
½ pound torchetti or other dried short pasta

Stir together the olives, parsley, capers, garlic, anchovies, preserved lemon, red pepper flakes, lemon juice, and olive oil in a large bowl. Season with salt and pepper, and set aside.

Cook the pasta in a large pot of boiling salted water over high heat until just tender, 10–12 minutes. Drain the pasta. Add the pasta to the bowl with the sauce and toss well. Adjust the seasonings. Serve warm or at room temperature.

Caponata

{ makes about 8 cups }

Make a generous batch of this chunky, olive-studded, Sicilian eggplant antipasto to have on hand—you'll be set for the week. It makes a wonderful lunch served with sliced prosciutto or any of the great Italian salami along with hard-boiled eggs, or spoon it over poached fish or chicken.

2 large eggplants, cut into 1-inch cubes
¼ cup kosher salt
½ cup red wine vinegar
1 tablespoon sugar
¼ cup dried currants or raisins
¾ cup olive oil
3 stalks celery, cut into large dice
1 medium onion, peeled and chopped
4 anchovy fillets, chopped
One 28-ounce can whole, peeled plum tomatoes, quartered, and their juices
1 cup large green olives, pitted and halved
2 tablespoons capers, drained
1 bay leaf
Freshly ground black pepper

SIMPLE TIP
This Sicilian classic is best served with a glass of Sicily's most well-known red wine, Nero d'Avola.

Toss the eggplant with the salt in a colander and let sit for about 1 hour to drain out the bitter liquid. Combine the vinegar and sugar in a small bowl. Add the currants and set aside to plump.

Pat the eggplant dry with paper towels. Heat ½ cup of the olive oil in a heavy, wide pot over medium-high heat. Working in batches, fry the eggplant until browned all over, about 10 minutes. Transfer the eggplant with a slotted spatula to a bowl.

Add the remaining ¼ cup olive oil, the celery, and the onions to the pot. Cook over medium heat until just soft, about 10 minutes. Stir in the anchovies. Add the tomatoes with their juices, the olives, capers, and bay leaf. Return the eggplant to the pot. Stir in the currants and vinegar. Simmer, stirring gently and often, until the juices thicken a bit, 10–15 minutes. Season with pepper. Refrigerate for at least one day and up to one week. Remove the bay leaf before serving.

4.

Cocktail Hour Bites

Pack big flavor into small bites

In the Mediterranean, cocktail hour (although it's usually longer) is a bridge between the end of the day and the typical late, but light dinner. Our cocktail bites, a twist on meze and tapas, are all about fun and informality. All are simple, shareable, and easy to prepare in advance.

Cocktail Banderillos

{ makes as many as you like }

These tapas, little Spanish skewers, are named after the decorated, colorful lance used in bullfighting, and are typically made with pickled or salty things, like olives, onions, carrots, and anchovies. They are the perfect small bite with a drink to whet your appetite. Try these combinations or make up your own.

Cut white country-style or artisan bread into ½-inch crustless bread cubes. Heat a little olive oil in a heavy skillet over medium heat. Toast the bread cubes, in a single layer, without crowding the skillet, until lighted browned all over, about 5 minutes. Transfer to a plate and season lightly with salt.

Marinated Beet, Olive & Quail Egg

Slide the ingredients onto a long, flat wooden cocktail toothpick in this order: ½ peeled hard-boiled quail egg, 1 pitted olive, ½-inch cube marinated beet, and 1 toasted bread cube.

Marinated Mushroom, Caperberry & Anchovy

Slide the ingredients onto a long, flat wooden cocktail toothpick in this order: 1 marinated mushroom, ¼ caperberry wrapped with 1 anchovy fillet, and 1 toasted bread cube.

Roasted Tomato, Serrano & Manchego

Slide the ingredients onto a long, flat wooden cocktail toothpick in this order: 1 piece roasted tomato, 1 rolled-up slice serrano ham, and a 1-inch cube of manchego cheese.

Pickled Garlic, Pepperoncini & Chorizo

Slide the ingredients onto a long, flat wooden cocktail toothpick in this order: 1 small clove pickled garlic, 1 small pepperoncini, and ½-inch-thick slice chorizo.

Olive, Olive & Olive

Slide the ingredients onto a long, flat wooden cocktail toothpick in this order: 2 stuffed olives, 1 pitted olive, and 1 toasted bread cube.

Belgian Endive with Marinated Artichoke Hearts & Shrimp

{ makes 8 }

We make this elegant salad of artichoke hearts and shrimp in advance and keep it in the fridge until it's time to spoon it into endive leaves for an easy hors d'oeuvre. To serve as a salad, toss with endive and bibb lettuce, or other tender greens.

Toss 8 small, peeled, cooked shrimp and 8 marinated artichoke heart quarters plus 2 tablespoons of their marinade with 1 tablespoon extra-virgin olive oil in a medium bowl. Season with salt and freshly ground black pepper. From 1 Belgian endive, remove 8 of the nicest leaves. To serve, place 1 shrimp and 1 piece of artichoke on the wide end of each endive leaf, then arrange the leaves on a serving platter. Garnish with thin lemon wedges.

Left (top to bottom):
Feta & Stuffed Olive Mash
Serrano Ham & Fig Spread
Sardines, Hearts of Palm &
Hard-Boiled Egg.
Right (top to bottom):
Brie & Cornichons
Blue Cheese & Stuffed Olive Mash
Blue Cheese & Orange Fig Spread

Little Toasts

We bake these crisp little toasts in advance so when guests drop by or we want an impromptu snack, we can quickly assemble them with any topping we have on hand. Here are a few suggestions to try.

Preheat the oven to 400°F. Slice a baguette or other crusty bread into small rounds or other shapes. Arrange the bread on a baking sheet, brush with extra-virgin olive oil, and toast in the oven, turning once, until browned on both sides, about 10 minutes. Store them in airtight containers, letting them first cool completely.

Feta & Stuffed Olive Mash

{ makes about ½ cup or enough for 8 toasts }

Mash together 4 tablespoons feta, 2 tablespoons chopped pitted olives, 2 tablespoons finely chopped parsley leaves, ¼ teaspoon grated lemon zest, and 2 tablespoons softened butter in a small bowl. Season with freshly ground black pepper. Spread the mash on little toasts or crackers and garnish with parsley.

Serrano Ham & Fig Spread

{ makes 1 }

Drape a little toast with a slice (or half a slice if a whole one is too big) of serrano ham. Top the toast with 1 teaspoon fig spread.

Sardines, Hearts of Palm & Hard-Boiled Egg

{ makes 1 }

Lay half a sardine on a little toast. Put 1 slice hard-boiled egg, 1 teaspoon diced, pickled heart of palm on top. Add a drop of extra-virgin olive oil. Season with salt and freshly ground black pepper. Garnish with pickled chile.

Brie & Cornichons

{ makes 1 }

Lay 1 small piece ripe Brie on a little toast or cracker. Top the toast with a halved cornichon.

Blue Cheese & Stuffed Olive Mash

{ makes about 2/3 cup or enough for 10 toasts }

Mash together 4 tablespoons Saga blue cheese, 4 tablespoons chopped citrus-stuffed olives and 2 tablespoons softened butter in a small bowl. Season to taste with freshly ground black pepper. Spread the mash on little toasts or crackers and garnish with chopped chives and a slice of olive.

Blue Cheese & Orange Fig Spread

{ makes 1 }

Spread a little toast with some Saga blue or other creamy blue cheese. Top the toast with 1 teaspoon orange fig spread. Season with freshly ground black pepper.

Roasted Olives

{ makes about 2 cups }

Roasting olives concentrates their flavors and the aromatics infuse the olive oil. We like to serve these olives as an hors d'oeuvre, and use the oil to dip warm, crusty bread. Use a selection of your favorite olives, with or without pits, for this simple, quick dish.

Preheat the oven to 425°F. Toss 2 cups olives, 1 lemon, sliced into thin rounds, 4 sprigs fresh thyme, 2 sprigs fresh rosemary, ½ teaspoon fennel seeds, and ¼ teaspoon crushed red pepper flakes with ½ cup extra-virgin olive oil in a medium roasting pan or baking dish. Roast the olives in the oven, stirring once or twice, until fragrant, about 20 minutes.

SIMPLE TIP

Who needs scented candles? Before company arrives, pop these in the oven to fill your house with an inviting aroma.

Polenta Toasts with
Olive Spread & Roasted Tomatoes

{ makes about 48 }

Freshly made polenta make these "toasts" particularly delicious—they can even be made from polenta left over from a previous meal.

¾ cup polenta
Salt
¾ cup grated Parmigiano-Reggiano
¼ cup extra-virgin olive oil plus 1 tablespoon
½ cup kalamata olive spread
16 pieces roasted tomatoes, cut into thirds

Put 4 cups cold water into a medium heavy-bottomed pot. Stir in the polenta and 1 generous pinch of salt. Bring to a boil over medium-high heat, stirring often. Reduce the heat to medium-low, and cook the polenta, stirring occasionally, until tender, about 45 minutes. The polenta will swell and thicken as it cooks. Stir in a little more water as needed if it gets too thick before it finishes cooking. Stir in the cheese and season with salt.

Oil an 8-inch square baking pan with 1 tablespoon of the olive oil. Spread the hot polenta in an even layer ½ inch thick in the pan, smoothing the top with a wet rubber spatula. Set aside to cool. Transfer to the refrigerator, uncovered, to firm up and cool completely.

Cut the polenta into 1-inch squares, discarding scraps. Heat the remaining ¼ cup oil in a nonstick skillet over medium heat until hot. Working in batches, fry the polenta squares until deep golden brown, about 2 minutes per side. Drain on paper towels.

To serve, top half of the polenta toasts with a small spoonful of olive spread and the remaining toasts with a piece of roasted tomato.

SIMPLE TIP
Short on time but want to try the recipe? Buy pre-cooked polenta at the market and cut it into rounds.

5.

Weeknight Dinners

Simple and delicious meals
for the family

These one-dish crowd pleasers use just a few ingredients and take only a minimal amount of time to prep and prepare. Served right from the pot or skillet, these dishes deliver the goods effortlessly, leaving you with plenty of time for relaxed, convivial evenings with your loved ones. It's our idea of family style!

Preserved Lemon Risotto

{ serves 4 }

Risotto, the beloved Italian rice dish, is traditionally made with pearly, short-grain rice cultivated in the northern Po valley. There are three common rice varieties—vialone nano, carnaroli, and arborio, the most widely available. The kernels, when cooked, have the remarkable ability to absorb up to five times their weight in liquid yet still retain their shape. A properly cooked risotto is moist, not soupy, the rice swollen with broth and just a bit chewy in the center. No wonder a warm dish of risotto is so soul-satisfying.

5 cups chicken or vegetable broth, or water
½ preserved lemon
4 tablespoons butter
1 small onion, peeled and finely chopped
1 clove garlic, peeled and minced
1 cup arborio rice
¼ cup white wine
½ cup grated Parmigiano-Reggiano
Salt
Freshly ground black pepper

Fill a medium pot with the broth, add the preserved lemon, and bring to a gentle simmer over medium heat. Reduce heat to low to keep the broth hot.

Melt 3 tablespoons of the butter in a heavy, wide pot over medium heat. Add the onions and cook, stirring with a wooden spoon, until soft but not browned, about 3 minutes. Add the garlic, then add the rice, stirring until everything is coated with butter. Pour in the wine and stir until the rice has absorbed it, about 2 minutes. Add 1 cup of the simmering broth, stirring constantly to keep the rice from sticking to the bottom of the pot. Push any rice that sticks to the sides back down into the liquid. When the rice has absorbed all the broth, add another cup of broth.

Continue in this way until you have added most of the broth, about 20 minutes. The rice is done when it is just tender and still a little soupy.

Remove the preserved lemon from the pot of broth and discard the pulp. Mince the rind and add it to the risotto.

Remove the risotto from the heat. Add the cheese and the remaining 1 tablespoon butter, stirring until it has melted into the rice. Season with salt and pepper, if needed.

Simply Mediterranean

Marinated Artichoke & Parsley Risotto

{ serves 4 }

Italians traditionally make a version of this dish in the springtime using fresh artichokes. We make this risotto all year long with big, meaty, marinated artichokes.

Follow the directions for risotto (page 96), omitting the preserved lemon and adding 3 chopped marinated artichokes with stems and ½ cup chopped parsley leaves to the rice after it has cooked for 20 minutes. Garnish each serving of risotto with a marinated artichoke half and a parsley leaf, if you like.

Shrimp & Roasted Tomato Risotto

{ serves 4 }

SIMPLE TIP
Risotto can be intimidating but the truth is that it only takes 30 minutes to make and is a great way to use the last of whatever fresh veggies may be in your fridge.

When we don't have shellfish or fish stock on hand to make this risotto, we put the shells from the shrimp in the simmering water to add a bit of flavor, then discard them.

Follow the directions for risotto (page 96), omitting the chicken broth and using water or shellfish or fish stock. Add 2 tablespoons tomato paste to the pot when adding the garlic. Add ¼ cup coarsely chopped, roasted tomatoes to the pot after the rice has cooked for 10 minutes. Gently stir 1 pound small, peeled, and deveined shrimp into the rice a few minutes before it is finished cooking. Omit the cheese.

Chicken Breasts with Gigandes Beans in Tomato Sauce

{ serves 2 }

The huge white beans aptly named gigandes (gigantes, Greek for giant), are similar to large white lima beans, but when cooked, are more plump and velvety. Grown in northern Greece, they are traditionally used for gigandes plaki, the tomatoey baked bean dish. We adore them plain, dressed with olive oil, lemon juice, and fresh herbs, or in tomato sauce, as we do here, served warm or at room temperature.

2 small boneless, skinless chicken breasts or 1 large breast, halved lengthwise
Salt
Freshly ground black pepper
1 tablespoon extra-virgin olive oil
2 cups gigandes beans in tomato sauce
1 cup basil leaves, torn into pieces
1 lemon, quartered

SIMPLE TIP
Traditionally seasoned with dill, Greek style tomato sauce is rich, with an oniony sweetness.

Season the chicken with salt and pepper. Heat the oil in a medium skillet over medium heat. Add the chicken, the smoother and flatter side down, and cook until pale golden brown, about 5 minutes. Turn the chicken over and cook the other side until the juices run clear when the meat is pierced, about 2 minutes. Transfer the chicken to a plate.

Discard the fat from the skillet and return the skillet to medium-low heat. Add the gigandes beans and basil, and season with pepper and a little salt, if you like. Cover and simmer until the beans are warmed through and the basil has wilted, 2–3 minutes. Divide the beans and sauce between two dinner plates, then set a chicken breast on top of each. Garnish with a drizzle of olive oil, some lemon, and a sprig of basil, if you like.

Chicken Thighs with Marinated Mushrooms

{ serves 2–4 }

The boneless, skinless chicken breast has its virtues, but when you want a flavorful, juicy piece of chicken with crisp skin, the thigh is what you're after. Thighs take longer to cook, but they are worth it. Cook them slowly, skin-side down, resisting the urge to move them. Eventually, the fat melts away and the skin becomes thin, golden brown, and crisp.

1 tablespoon olive oil
4 chicken thighs
Salt
Freshly ground black pepper
1½ cups marinated mushrooms and garlic

Put the oil into a large skillet over medium heat. Season the chicken with salt and pepper and add to the skillet, skin-side down. Cook the thighs, without moving them, until the skin is browned and crisp, 20–30 minutes. Reduce the heat to medium-low if the skin begins to burn before it becomes evenly browned.

Turn the thighs over and add the mushrooms, nestling them in between the chicken. Continue cooking the thighs until the juices from the meat closest to the bone run clear when the meat is pierced, about 15 minutes.

Chicken Thighs with Kale & Alfonso Olives

{ serves 2–4 }

We love the large, plump, and meaty Alfonso olive for this dish. The rich chicken thighs are a good foil for the delicate brininess of these olives. If Alfonso is not available, choose another briny variety, such as Kalamata or blond Mt. Pelion.

Follow the above directions for the chicken thighs, cooking them in the skillet until the skin is crisp and golden, 20–30 minutes. Transfer them to a plate and set aside. Add 1 large bunch kale, leaves stripped from the stems and the center rib or 4 cups kale leaves to the skillet. Cover and cook, turning the leaves as they cook, until wilted, about 15 minutes. Add 1¼ cups Alfonso olives. Return the thighs to the skillet, skin-side up, nestling them in between the kale and olives. Cook until the thighs are cooked through and the kale is tender, about 15 minutes.

Pasta with Pesto & Zucchini

{ serves 4–6 }

This pasta dish is inspired by the Ligurian Trofie al Pesto (gnocchi with pesto) which includes thin green beans and cubes of cooked potatoes. Use the smallest zucchini you can find. They have fewer seeds and hold their pretty round shape when cooked and tossed with the pesto.

3–4 small zucchini, cut crosswise into ½-inch-thick rounds
1¼ cups pesto
1 pound campanelle or other short pasta
1 cup freshly grated Parmigiano-Reggiano
Salt
Freshly ground black pepper

Bring a large pot of salted water to a boil over high heat. Blanch the zucchini in the boiling water until just tender, 2–3 minutes. Scoop the zucchini out of the water with a slotted spoon and transfer to a medium bowl. Add ¼ cup of the pesto and toss well.

SIMPLE TIP
Always add pesto off the heat to keep it from separating.

Add the pasta to the pot of boiling water and cook, stirring often, until just tender, about 10 minutes. Drain the pasta, reserving ½ cup of the pasta water. Put the pasta in a large bowl and toss with the remaining 1 cup pesto. Add the cheese, toss well, and add some of the reserved pasta water to loosen the sauce. Add the zucchini and toss well. Season with salt and pepper.

Orecchiette with Marinated Chickpeas, Dill & Lemon Zest

{ serves 4 }

There are other short pasta shapes that could be used for this dish, but orecchiette, named for its dimpled round shape resembling small ears, is suited to cup the chickpeas perfectly.

½ pound orecchiette pasta
1 cup Mediterranean chickpeas in marinade
2 tablespoons extra-virgin olive oil
2–3 tablespoons chopped fresh dill
1 lemon
Salt
Freshly ground black pepper

Bring a large pot of salted water to a boil over high heat. Add the pasta and cook, stirring often, until just tender, 8–10 minutes. Drain the pasta.

Put the pasta in a large bowl. Add chickpeas, olive oil, and dill. Finely grate the zest of the lemon over the pasta. Add the juice from half of the lemon. Season with salt and pepper. Toss well, adjust the seasonings, and serve.

Salad Niçoise

{ serves 2 }

This salad, inspired by the famous one from southern France, relies in part on the goodness of these two ingredients: small, earthy Niçoise olives and the best-quality tuna (look for ventrèche de thon) packed in olive oil.

Everyday Vinaigrette (page 23)
½ preserved lemon, rind only
4 small waxy potatoes, boiled, cooled, and quartered
½ pound string beans, trimmed, boiled, and cooled
One 6-ounce jar tuna packed in olive oil, drained
6 small tomatoes, cored and halved
3 hard-boiled eggs, peeled and halved
½ cup Niçoise olives
Parsley sprigs for garnish, optional

Put the vinaigrette in a small bowl. Slice the preserved lemon rind into strips. Set 2 strips aside for garnish. Chop the remaining strips and add them to the vinaigrette.

SIMPLE TIP
Authentic Niçoise olives may be difficult to find but can easily be swapped with Coquillos, their counterpart from Spain.

Arrange the potatoes, string beans, tuna, tomatoes, and hard-boiled eggs on a serving platter. Scatter the olives around the salad. Garnish the tuna with the reserved preserved lemon strips and the salad with parsley sprigs, if you like. Dress the salad with the vinaigrette just before serving.

Avocado Toast

{ makes 4 }

There are few things we love to eat as much as perfectly ripe avocados. Especially when the buttery flesh is spread on toast and anointed with olive oil. We could (and do) eat these for breakfast, lunch, dinner, and any time in between. Choose unripe, firm avocados and let them ripen at room temperature away from direct sunlight. Gently squeeze the avocado. It is ripe when it yields to firm, gentle pressure. Avocados keep well in the refrigerator.

4 slices crusty bread
1 clove garlic, peeled
Extra-virgin olive oil
2 ripe Hass avocados, halved, pitted, and peeled
1 lemon, halved
Salt
Crushed red pepper flakes

Toast the bread, rub one side with the raw garlic to flavor it, then drizzle the garlicky side with some olive oil.

Put the avocados into a wide bowl and mash them with a fork until smooth. Spread the avocado mash on the toast. Drizzle with more olive oil. Squeeze lemon juice on top, and season with salt and red pepper flakes.

SIMPLE TIP
This is a great recipe to let the family customize with their favorite toppings like roasted tomatoes, a soft boiled egg, fresh basil, or cilantro.

Grilled Cheese
with Roasted Tomatoes

{ makes 1 }

For this comforting sandwich, we like to use a good melting cheese, like an aged Cheddar or Fontina Val d'Aosta, to contrast with the deep, rich flavor of the roasted tomatoes.

1–2 tablespoons butter, at room temperature
2 slices artisanal bread
¾ cup grated Cheddar, Fontina, or other melting cheese
4–8 pieces roasted tomatoes, drained

Butter one side of each slice of bread. This will be the side that gets grilled. Turn one slice over and cover with half of the cheese. Arrange the tomatoes over the cheese, then cover with the remaining cheese. Put the sandwich together with the buttered sides facing out. Set the sandwich aside.

SIMPLE TIP
A few standout savory grilled cheese combinations: mushrooms and Gruyère, roasted peppers and goat cheese or zucchini and fresh mozzarella.

Heat a medium skillet over medium-low heat. Add the sandwich and cook until the cheese melts and each side is golden brown, 2–3 minutes per side. Cut in half and serve.

114

Grilled Cheese & Sour Cherry Spread Sandwich

{ makes 1 }

Sometimes we forget how satisfying a grilled cheese sandwich can be for dinner. Treat yourself to a couple of these savory-sweet cheese toasts, served with a leafy salad and a glass of wine, if you like. It's a meal that could easily become a habit.

1–2 tablespoons butter, at room temperature
2 slices artisanal bread
2 tablespoons sour cherry spread
¾ cup grated Gruyère cheese
Freshly ground black pepper, optional

Spread the butter on one side of each slice of bread and slather the other side with the cherry spread. Cover the cherry spread with the cheese on one slice of bread. Close the sandwich with the other slice of bread, butter-side up. Set the sandwich aside.

Heat a medium skillet over medium-low heat. Add the sandwich and cook until the cheese melts and the crust is golden brown, 2–3 minutes on each side. Transfer the sandwich to a cutting board and season with pepper, if you like. Cut in half and serve.

SIMPLE TIP
Some sweet combinations we adore: fig spread and brie or hazelnut spread with strawberries and mascarpone.

6.

Gatherings

Antipasti platters &
easy entertaining

For a taste of Italy, Greece, Spain, or France, our regionally inspired antipasti platters are the perfect way to impress a crowd, large or small. Each shines with little bites: olives, charcuterie, marinated vegetables and beans, regional cheeses, artisan breads, tapenades, dips, and spreads. You can assemble these in a few minutes before your friends arrive and watch as the delicious morsels disappear.

If you want to move on to a hot course, we've included some of our favorite shareable platters to complete the feast!

THE GREEK ISLES
Pita bread, roasted red
peppers, pepperoncini,
mixed Greek olives
(Kalamata, Mt. Athos,
Gordal), tzatziki with
fresh cucumber, dolmas
(stuffed grape leaves),
Greek feta drizzled
with EVOO and fresh
oregano, marinated
beets, gigandes beans in
vinaigrette.

ITALIAN ANTIPASTO MISTO

Prosciutto, marinated mushrooms, rosemary focaccia, Castelvetrano olives, fresh mozzarella topped with roasted tomatoes and basil, breadsticks, cherry peppers stuffed with prosciutto and provolone, long-stem artichokes, Cerignola olives (green and black), grilled artichokes, arancini (stuffed rice balls),

A TASTE OF FRANCE
French cocktail olives
with lupini beans and
peppers, Niçoise olives,
black olive spread,
ham, fresh baguette
and butter topped with,
fleur de sel, whole grain
mustard, Lucque olives,
cornichons, pâté.

FLAVORS OF SPAIN
Chorizo, olive oil tortas,
marinated chickpeas,
Arbequina olives, piquillo
peppers, tuna packed in EVOO
topped with preserved lemon,
membrillo (quince paste),
manchego, p'tit brebis,
Marcona almonds, artichoke
quarters in herbs, caperberries.

Risotto-Stuffed Piquillo Peppers

{ makes 16-24 }

These are a delicious way to use up leftover risotto. Approximately 3 tablespoons risotto will fill a piquillo pepper. If stuffing the peppers with just-made risotto, let the risotto cool to room temperature. It will firm up, hold its shape, and won't spill out of the stuffed pepper.

16–24 piquillo peppers
1 recipe risotto (page 96-99) of your choice, cool or at room temperature
Extra-virgin olive oil
Parsley, for garnish

Preheat the oven to 350°F. Carefully fill the cavity of each piquillo pepper with some risotto. Arrange the stuffed peppers in a roasting pan drizzled with olive oil. Bake the peppers until warmed through, about 30 minutes. Serve the peppers garnished with parsley, if you like.

SIMPLE TIP
Piquillo peppers are named for their shape (Piquillo translates to "little beak") and can be stuffed with anything from tuna to chorizo to goat cheese.

Tomato & Olive Tart

{ serves 4–6 }

Puff pastry, the flaky French dough, is available in sheets in the freezer section of most grocery stores. Choose a brand that is made with butter—ones made with vegetable shortening sorely lack flavor.

1 sheet puff pastry, defrosted
Flour
2–3 tomatoes, cored and sliced
½ cup olives, pitted and halved lengthwise
Extra-virgin olive oil
Freshly ground black pepper
Salt

Preheat the oven to 375°F. Line a large baking sheet with a piece of parchment paper and set aside. Roll the puff pastry out on a lightly floured surface into a ¼-inch-thick rectangle the shape of the baking sheet. Transfer the sheet of puff pastry to the parchment paper–lined baking sheet. Using the tip of a paring knife, lightly score a border about ½ inch from the edge of the pastry. Prick the dough within the border all over with a fork to prevent it from puffing up too much during baking.

Arrange the tomatoes on the pastry in a single layer (do not crowd or overlap the tomatoes or the puff pastry will be soggy). Arrange the olives on top of the tomatoes. Drizzle the tart with olive oil and season with pepper.

Bake the tart until the pastry is crisp and deeply browned on the bottom and around the edges, 30–40 minutes. Remove from oven, season with salt, and serve.

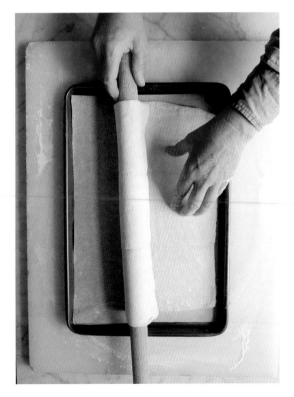

Simply Mediterranean

134   Simply Mediterranean

Artichoke Hearts & Zucchini Frittata

{ serves 6–8 }

The beauty of making a frittata, the popular Italian omelet, is how quick and simple it is to put together for a meal for two or a large gathering. Layer it with any number of vegetable, cheese, and/or cured meat combinations, like a quiche, but no pastry-making skills are needed. We serve frittatas like this one, with tender zucchini, onions, and zesty artichokes at any meal. They always hit the spot.

2 tablespoons extra-virgin olive oil
1 onion, peeled and sliced
2 zucchini, trimmed and cut into thick pieces
2 cups marinated artichoke hearts, drained
8 cloves pickled garlic, halved lengthwise
½ preserved lemon, rind only, cut into thin strips
8 eggs
1–2 pinches of salt
Pinch of crushed red pepper flakes
⅓–½ cup grated Parmigiano-Reggiano

SIMPLE TIP
Frittatas are a great way to help use up your leftover greens, vegetables, and cheeses.

Set the oven rack in the middle of the oven and preheat the broiler to high. Heat the oil in a large ovenproof skillet over medium heat. Add the onions and cook, stirring often, until soft, about 5 minutes. Add the zucchini and cook, stirring often, until it begins to soften, about 5 minutes. Scatter the artichokes, garlic, and preserved lemon strips around the onions and garlic.

Beat the eggs, salt, red pepper flakes, and a splash of water together in a medium bowl. Pour the eggs over the vegetables in the skillet. Cook over medium heat until the eggs begin to set around the edge and the center is still runny, about 10 minutes. Scatter the cheese over the eggs.

Transfer the skillet to the oven and broil the frittata until the cheese is melted and the top is golden brown, 8–10 minutes. Serve warm or at room temperature.

Roasted Salmon with Brussels Sprouts & Green Olives

{ serves 8–10 }

When we are planning a menu for a large gathering, we often choose dishes that can be enjoyed at room temperature. That way, once the table is set, our kitchen duties are over and we can relax with our guests. A whole side of salmon, roasted or grilled, and this rustic toss of Brussels sprouts and olives are two of our favorites, served together or separately.

FOR THE SALMON
1 whole side salmon fillet, pin bones removed
2 tablespoons extra-virgin olive oil, plus more for drizzling
Salt
Freshly ground black pepper
2 lemons, cut into 8–10 wedges
Parsley sprigs for garnish, optional

FOR THE BRUSSELS SPROUTS
4 pounds Brussels sprouts, trimmed and halved lengthwise
½ pound pancetta, diced
4–6 tablespoons extra-virgin olive oil
2 cups pitted green olives
1 teaspoon crushed red pepper flakes
Salt
Freshly ground black pepper

For the salmon, set the oven rack in the middle of the oven and preheat the oven to 400°F. Lay the salmon skin-side down on a large sheet pan lined with parchment paper. Rub the flesh side of the fish with 2 tablespoons of the olive oil and season well with salt and pepper.

Roast the salmon in the oven until just cooked through, 20–25 minutes. To test for doneness, slip the tip of a paring knife into the center of the thickest part of the fish. Remove the knife and quickly (and carefully) press it to your lower lip. If it is very warm the fish is cooked. Let the salmon cool to room temperature.

For the Brussels sprouts, increase the oven temperature to 450°F. Bring a large pot of salted water to a boil over high heat. Working in batches, blanch the Brussels sprouts in the boiling water for 1 minute. Transfer them with a slotted spoon to a colander to drain.

Put the pancetta and 2 tablespoons of the olive oil in a large skillet and cook over medium heat until the pancetta is browned, about 5 minutes. Transfer the pancetta with a slotted spoon to a large roasting pan. Working in batches to avoid crowding, cook the Brussels sprouts in the skillet, stirring often, until just tender, about 10 minutes. Transfer the Brussels sprouts to the roasting pan with the pancetta.

Add the olives to the Brussels sprouts in the roasting pan and drizzle with more olive oil, if you like. Season with the red pepper flakes, salt, and pepper. Stir well. Transfer the pan to the oven and roast the Brussels sprouts until tender and the leaves begin to char, 20–30 minutes. Let the Brussels sprouts cool to room temperature.

Serve the Brussels sprouts on a platter and the salmon on another platter, drizzled with more olive oil, and garnished with lemon wedges, and parsley, if you like.

Simply Mediterranean

Grilled Lamb Chops
& Radicchio with Pickled Garlic

{ *serves 8–12* }

A big platter of smoky grilled lamb chops, charry on the outside, rosy in the center, is irresistible. Guests always try to sneak a chop or two before the meal is served. Let the grilled lamb rest until you are ready to serve it, warm or at room temperature, then slice it into individual chops—that way the meat will stay pink longer.

Four 8-rib racks of lamb, frenched
Extra-virgin olive oil
Freshly ground black pepper
Salt
2 heads radicchio, quartered lengthwise
2–3 bunches scallions, trimmed
12 pieces pickled garlic, halved lengthwise
3 lemons, quartered

Prepare a medium-hot fire to one side of a charcoal grill. If using a gas grill, fire up the "back burner" to medium-hot heat.

Cut each rack of lamb in half into 4-rib pieces. Rub the chops all over with a little olive oil, and season well with salt and pepper.

Grill the lamb in the center of the grill, moving it to a cooler spot if there are flare-ups. Turn the pieces as they brown. When the meat has a nice brown crust all over, move it to the coolest spot on the grill to finish cooking, turning it occasionally, until the internal temperature reaches 125°F for medium-rare. The grilling time will vary depending on the grill and the heat. Transfer the lamb to a cutting board, loosely cover with foil, and allow it to rest briefly.

Lightly coat the radicchio and scallions with olive oil, and season with salt and pepper. Grill the radicchio and scallions, turning them as they brown, until the radicchio is wilted and the scallions are tender, about 10 minutes. Transfer the vegetables to a serving platter. Scatter with the garlic. Drizzle with olive oil. Season with salt and pepper.

Cut the lamb ribs into individual chops, pile them on a large platter, drizzle with olive oil, and season with salt and pepper. Garnish the platter with lemon wedges. Serve with the radicchio, scallions, and garlic.

A SWEET FINISH
For dessert, arrange
a platter of seasonal
fruits, berries, and
melon.

7.

Weekend Favorites

Relaxed meals for friends and family

La dolce vita.

Mostly inspired by the cuisine of Italy, where *abbondanza* and good food are inseparable, our weekend meals will delight a small group of friends or family. Plus, they're so easy to prepare, you'll have all the time in the world to simply relax and enjoy.

Simply Mediterranean

Pappardelle with Wild Mushrooms

{ serves 6–8 }

Pappardelle, the wide ribbonlike pasta, is available fresh or dried. We use the dried pasta for hearty, stewy sauces, but for this more delicate dish, we prefer the silkiness of fresh pasta.

1 pound fresh pappardelle
2 cups wild mushroom mix in olive oil, drained
1 cup parsley leaves, chopped
2 tablespoons extra-virgin olive oil
Zest of 1 lemon
Freshly squeezed lemon juice, to taste
Salt
Freshly ground black pepper
Parmigiano-Reggiano

Bring a large pot of salted water to a boil over high heat. Add the pasta and cook, stirring often, until just tender. Drain the pasta, reserving some of the cooking water.

Return the pasta to the pot over low heat. Add the mushrooms, parsley, and olive oil, and toss well. Add the lemon zest to the pasta, and add freshly squeezed lemon juice to taste. Season with salt and pepper. Loosen the sauce with some of the reserved cooking water, if you like. Serve warm with lots of freshly grated Parmigiano-Reggiano.

Wild Mushroom & Fontina Pizza

{ makes one 10-inch pizza }

We enjoy making pizza at home. We set out a variety of toppings and let everyone choose their own combination. It's a fun way to gather in the kitchen and make something delicious together. Bakeries that make pizza and/or focaccia often sell excellent pizza dough, and balls of dough can also be found in the freezer section of most grocery stores.

½ pound pizza dough
Flour
Cornmeal
Extra-virgin olive oil
1 cup grated Fontina cheese
2 cups wild mushroom mix in olive oil, drained
Crushed red pepper flakes

Preheat the oven to 500°F and place a pizza stone on the upper rack.

Shape the dough into a ball on a lightly floured surface. Stretch the dough into a 10-inch round, letting it rest and relax between stretches, if resistant. Lay the dough out on a cornmeal-dusted pizza peel or a rimless baking sheet. Prick the surface with a fork and brush with olive oil.

Scatter the grated cheese over the dough, and top with the mushrooms. Season with red pepper flakes.

Slide the pizza off the peel onto the hot pizza stone in the oven. Bake until the crust is puffed and golden around the edges and the topping is bubbling hot, 6–8 minutes. Use the peel to remove the pizza from the oven. Cut the pizza into wedge and serve.

Simply Mediterranean

Gorgonzola, Fig Spread & Walnut Pizza

{ makes one 10-inch pizza }

To add a savory note to this luscious pizza, consider draping it with slices of prosciutto when the pizza comes out of the oven.

Follow the directions for pizza (page 150), substituting ½ cup crumbled gorgonzola for the Fontina, 6–8 teaspoons orange fig spread for the mushrooms, and freshly ground black pepper for the crushed red pepper flakes. Arrange 12 shelled walnut halves over the pizza and bake until bubbling hot, 6–8 minutes.

SIMPLE TIP

Fruit preserves are a great base for appetizer or dessert pizzas. Another combination we love is sour cherry spread with chèvre and pecans.

Grilled Swordfish with Olives, Roasted Tomatoes & Caperberries

{ serves 4–8 }

Tear-shaped caperberries are the fruit of the caper bush. (Capers, incidentally, are the little flower buds of the same shrub.) Pickled caperberries, with their tiny seeds, add a little crunch and a bright note to this flavorful dish.

1 large tomato, halved
1 cup mixed olives
½ cup roasted tomatoes
12 caperberries, stemmed and halved
2 cloves pickled garlic, thinly sliced
¼ cup extra-virgin olive oil, plus 1 tablespoon for the fish
Freshly ground black pepper
Four 12-ounce swordfish steaks
Salt

SIMPLE TIP
Giving capers or caperberries a quick soak in water is a great way to reduce some of the saltiness.

One at a time, press the cut side of the tomato against the large holes on a box grater and grate the flesh into a medium saucepan, discarding the skins. Add the olives, roasted tomatoes, caperberries, garlic, and ¼ cup of the olive oil. Season with pepper. Simmer the sauce over medium heat for 5 minutes. Set the sauce aside.

Heat a large grill pan over medium-high heat. Rub the swordfish all over with the remaining 1 tablespoon olive oil and season with salt and pepper. Grill the swordfish in the hot pan until well marked and the fish is just cooked through, 6–8 minutes per side. You can also grill the swordfish over a hot charcoal grill, if you like.

Transfer the swordfish to a serving platter. Spoon the sauce over the fish. Serve warm or at room temperature.

Simply Mediterranean

Grilled Flatiron Steak with Green Olive & Hard-Boiled Egg Mash

{ serves 8 }

The flatiron or top blade steak is a long, medium-thick cut from the front shoulder, surprisingly tender and full of flavor, perfect for grilling. We keep the seasoning simple here, so the rich, piquant olive and egg mash can shine through.

FOR THE OLIVE AND EGG MASH
6 hard-boiled eggs, peeled and chopped
1 cup pitted green olives, chopped
1 cup parsley leaves, chopped
3 tablespoons capers, drained
2–3 tablespoons extra-virgin olive oil
Salt
Freshly ground black pepper

FOR THE STEAK
2 flatiron steaks
2 tablespoons extra-virgin olive oil, plus more for drizzling
Salt
Freshly ground black pepper

SIMPLE TIP
If you have leftover egg mash, have it for lunch the next day stuffed in a pita with sliced tomato and leafy greens.

For the olive and egg mash, mix the eggs, olives, parsley, and capers together in a medium bowl. Stir in the olive oil. Season with salt and pepper. Set the mash aside.

For the steak, prepare a hot charcoal or gas grill. Meanwhile, rub the steaks all over with the olive oil and season well with salt and pepper.

Grill the steaks over the hottest section of coals, turning them as they brown. When the meat has a nice brown crust all over, move it to the coolest spot on the grill to finish cooking, turning it occasionally, until the internal temperature reaches 120°F for rare or 130°F for medium-rare. The grilling time will vary depending on the grill and the heat. Transfer the steaks to a cutting board, loosely cover with foil, and let them rest for about 15 minutes. Slice the steaks, drizzle with a little olive oil, and serve with the olive and egg mash on the side.

Pound Cake with Kirsch & Sour Cherry Spread

{ make as many as you like }

We serve this simple combination—cake and jam—for dessert. When we have leftover pound cake, we sometimes have it for breakfast—a slice of the cake toasted and spread with lots of salty butter and sour cherry spread.

Sprinkle a slice of your favorite pound cake with a few drops of kirschwasser. Spread the cake with sour cherry spread to suit your taste. Serve on a dessert plate with a dollop of whipped cream.

Sour Cherry Granita

{ makes about 4 cups }

We like to serve this refreshing jewel-like granita with a delicate cookie or biscotti at the end of a meal, or as a pick-me-up treat in the afternoon.

SIMPLE TIP
A glass of sherry is an elegant complement to either of these desserts.

2 cups black cherry juice
½ cup sour cherry spread
Sweetened whipped cream

Put the cherry juice, sour cherry spread, and 1 cup water into a medium bowl and stir until the spread dissolves. Pour the cherry mixture into a pan (about 9 × 13 inches) or a wide container that will fit on a shelf in the freezer. Slide the pan into the freezer.

The liquid will become slushy-frozen in 3–4 hours. Scrape the granita with the tines of a fork, making frozen icy crystals throughout. Return the granita to the freezer to finish freezing, 3–4 hours. Give the granita a final scrape, breaking up any icy chunks with a fork. Serve small portions in chilled glasses with a big spoonful of whipped cream on top.

Fig Spread Tart with Sliced Almonds & Chocolate

Preheat the oven to 375°F. Lay 1 defrosted sheet of puff pastry out on a parchment paper–lined baking sheet. Using the tip of a paring knife, lightly score a border about ½ inch from the edge of the pastry. Prick the dough within the border all over with a fork to prevent it from puffing up too much during baking.

Spread 1 cup fig and orange spread in an even layer over the pastry. Scatter ½ cup sliced almonds on top. Bake the tart until well browned around the edges, about 30 minutes. Grate about 1 ounce bittersweet chocolate over the tart while still warm.

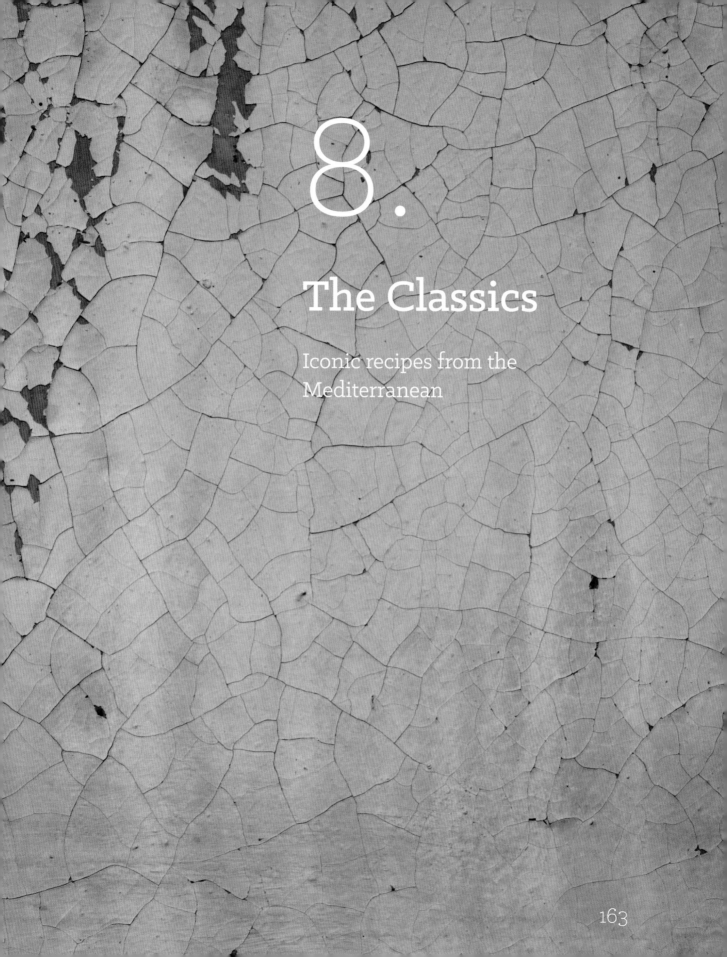

8.

The Classics

Iconic recipes from the Mediterranean

Each Mediterranean country has certain dishes that are deeply rooted in its culture. For us, these classics represent the essence of a region's culinary heritage and are the ultimate expression of people, place, and taste. In their ethereal ability to transport us to another time and place, these dishes are true Mediterranean masterpieces!

Garlic & Lemon Roasted Chicken with Black Olive Spread Toasts

{ serves 8–12 }

Provence, on the southeastern coast of France, is olive country—the gnarly trees are as integral to its rugged, sun-drenched landscape as fruit and oil are to its traditional cuisine. One of our favorite Provençal preparations is tapenade, the black olive paste mixed with capers, garlic, and olive oil that, spread on toast, is served as an hors d'oeuvre. This flavorful roast chicken, served with garlic-rubbed toasts slathered with black olive spread, is inspired by the bold flavors of Provence and its love of the olive.

FOR THE CHICKEN
2 whole chickens (3–5 pounds), rinsed and patted dry
½ cup extra-virgin olive oil
Salt
Freshly ground black pepper
2 lemons, halved
1 bunch fresh thyme
4–6 cloves garlic, unpeeled

FOR THE TOASTS
12 slices good country bread
2 cloves garlic, peeled
½ cup extra-virgin olive oil
1½ cups black olive spread
Crushed red pepper flakes
1 bunch fresh thyme

For the chicken, place an oven rack in the top third of the oven. Preheat the oven to 500°F. Put the chickens breast-side up in a large, heavy roasting pan. Rub the birds all over with 2–3 tablespoons of the olive oil and season inside and out with salt and pepper. Stuff each cavity with half a lemon and half the bunch of thyme. Tie the legs together with kitchen string. Tuck the wings under the back. Squeeze the juice of the remaining lemon halves over the birds and put the squeezed halves in the roasting pan with the chickens. Add the garlic and ½ cup water to the pan. Drizzle the chickens with a little more olive oil.

Roast the chickens until the skin is golden and taut, about 30 minutes. Reduce the oven temperature to 350°F. Continue roasting the birds until the skin is deep golden brown and the thigh juices run clear when pierced, about 30 minutes.

Transfer the chickens to a serving platter. Squeeze the garlic cloves out of their skins into the pan and mash into the pan juices. Discard the skins. Pour the pan juices into a gravy dish, and skim off the fat. Let the chickens rest for 15 minutes before carving.

For the toasts, toast the bread. Lightly rub the toasts with the garlic, then drizzle with a little olive oil. Spread the olive spread over the toasts. Drizzle on a little more olive oil. Arrange the toasts on a serving platter and season with the red pepper flakes. Scatter some thyme leaves on top and garnish the platter with the remaining thyme, if you like. Serve with the roast chicken.

Roast Leg of Lamb
with Wild Oregano & Dolmas

{ serves 8–12 }

Inspired by the celebratory feast of traditional Greek Easter, we have, on special occasions, spit-roasted whole lamb outside, swabbing the meat with lemon, oregano, and olive oil as it slowly roasts over hot coals of fragrant wood. Nothing tastes quite like it. Throughout the year, we more often roast a leg of lamb in the oven like we do here, and serve it with plenty of Greek meze, including one of our favorites, *dolmas* or *dolmades*, the tender rice-stuffed grape leaves.

1 whole leg of lamb, about 8 pounds
4 tablespoons extra-virgin olive oil
Salt
Freshly ground black pepper
1 bunch dried wild oregano
2 lemons, cut into sixths
32–48 dolmas (stuffed grape leaves)

SIMPLE TIP
If you find a whole leg intimidating, ask your butcher for a butterflied boneless leg and follow the same directions as above.

Preheat the oven to 350°F. Put the lamb into a large, heavy roasting pan, meatier-side up. Rub the leg all over with 2 tablespoons of the olive oil. Season generously with salt and pepper. Scatter the oregano over the lamb and around the pan. Drizzle the lamb with the remaining 2 tablespoons olive oil. Pour ½ cup water into the pan.

Roast the lamb until it is nicely browned on the outside, rosy pink on the inside, and the internal temperature reaches 130°F for medium-rare, 1–1½ hours. Transfer the lamb to a warm serving platter or cutting board, loosely tent it with foil, and let it rest for 15–20 minutes before carving. Pour the pan juices into a gravy dish and skim off the fat.

Arrange the dolmas on a serving platter and garnish with a slice of lemon, if you like. Garnish the lamb with the lemon wedges and serve the lamb with the pan juices and dolmas.

172

Paella

{ serves 8 }

Spain's traditional saffron-flecked rice dish, named for the wide metal pan it is cooked in, originated in Valencia, the eastern coastal city. Rice, first cultivated by the Moors, has been grown here in the Albufera lagoon for more than 1,300 years. Though rice is the real hero of a good paella, any number of ingredients can be added to give it the taste you want. Sometimes we add chicken, and/or mussels and shrimp, or splurge and make one with lobster and peas. If cooking a paella over an open fire or grill is out of the question, start it on top of the stove and finish cooking it in a preheated 375°F oven.

½ cup extra-virgin olive oil
2 onions, peeled and chopped
1–2 cloves garlic, peeled and chopped
4 cups Bomba, or arborio rice
2–3 pinches of saffron threads, lightly toasted in a skillet
16 cups warm clam or chicken broth, or water
Salt
8 ounces mild or hot Spanish chorizo, thinly sliced
50 littleneck clams, scrubbed
16–20 piquillo peppers, drained
1 bunch parsley, leaves chopped
2 lemons, quartered

Light a charcoal fire or gas grill. Make sure the paella pan fits comfortably on top of the grill. You want even, consistent heat under the whole pan.

Set the paella pan over the hot coals. Add the olive oil, using enough to thinly coat the entire surface of the pan. Add the onions and garlic, and cook, stirring often, until they begin to brown, about 2 minutes.

Stir in the rice. Crush the saffron threads between your fingers and add them to the hot broth. Generously season the broth with salt. Add about three-quarters of the broth to the pan, making sure everything in the pan is well distributed. Scatter the chorizo and clams over the rice. Arrange the piquillo peppers on top.

Cook the paella, rotating the pan for even cooking. **Do not stir it again**. You want the rice to develop a deep brown crust, or *socarrat,* on the bottom of the pan. Let the paella bubble away and cook until the rice is tender and the clams have opened (discard any shells that don't open). Test the rice for tenderness and pour more broth over the paella if the liquid evaporates before the rice is cooked.

Once the rice is tender, let the paella continue to cook a bit longer, ensuring that the rice absorbs all the liquid. When a brown crust has formed on the bottom of the pan (take a peek) and the edges of the paella begin to dry out and get crusty, the paella is done. The rice takes about 30 minutes to cook.

Scatter the parsley over the paella and garnish it with the lemon wedges. Remove the paella from the fire and cover it with a clean dishcloth to rest for 15 minutes or so before serving.

SIMPLE TIP
Invite your closest friends and family and eat straight from the pan as they do in Valencia!

Bistecca alla Fiorentina
& Cannellini Beans

{ serves 8 }

This classic Tuscan dish is for steak lovers only. The Florentines traditionally favor a very thick (2½- to 3-inches) T-bone or porterhouse cut from the grass-fed Tuscan Chianina breed of cattle for this dish. It is cooked over wood coals. It is served very rare, sometimes drizzled with their fine olive oil, sometimes served with their beloved cannellini beans. We use the best meat available, and prime grade when our wallet permits.

FOR THE BEANS
1 pound dried cannellini beans, soaked for 2–4 hours
3–4 sprigs fresh sage
2–3 very small dried red chiles
½ cup extra-virgin olive oil
Salt

FOR THE STEAK
One 2½-3-inch-thick T-bone or porterhouse steak
Extra-virgin olive oil, optional
Salt
Freshly ground black pepper, optional

For the beans, put the beans and their soaking water into a heavy, medium pot. Make sure they are covered by 2 inches of water, adding more water if necessary. Add the sage and chiles. Bring the beans just to a simmer over medium heat, stirring occasionally. Reduce the heat to low and very gently simmer them until they are plump and tender, 30–90 minutes, depending on their freshness.

Remove the pot from the heat. Drain off all but about ½ inch of the cooking water. Add the olive oil and season with salt. The beans can be served warm or at room temperature.

For the steak, prepare a hot wood or charcoal grill. Grill the steak over the hottest section of coals, turning it once it has developed a good brown crust, 5–7 minutes. Grill the second side for 5–7 minutes. Move the steak to a cooler spot on the grill if there are flare-ups. It should be cooked only until very rare, but you may prefer to cook it a little longer. Transfer the steak to a cutting board and drizzle with olive oil, if you like. Season with salt and pepper. Allow the steak to rest for about 15 minutes. Carve the strip and the tenderloin portions of the steak away from the bone, then thickly slice the meat. Serve with the beans.

Chicken Tagine with Chickpeas, Olives & Preserved Lemon

{ serves 8 }

This brothy, aromatic North African stew is named for the dish it is traditionally cooked in.

4 cloves garlic, peeled and mashed to a paste
½ teaspoon ground cumin
½ teaspoon ground ginger
½ teaspoon paprika
½ teaspoon turmeric
2 pinches of saffron threads
½ teaspoon salt
Freshly ground black pepper
1 whole chicken, rinsed, patted dry, and cut into 8–10 pieces
3 tablespoons extra-virgin olive oil
2 onions, peeled and sliced
4 cups chickpeas in Mediterranean marinade
2 preserved lemons, rind only, sliced
½ cup dry-cured black Beldi olives
½ cup hot Tunisian mixed olives, including the bay leaves, chiles, and onions
2–3 cinnamon sticks
1 cup chicken broth or water

Combine the garlic, cumin, ginger, paprika, turmeric, saffron, salt, and pepper to taste in a wide dish. Rub the spice paste all over the pieces of chicken. Cover and refrigerate for about 4 hours.

Set an oven rack in the lower part of the oven and preheat the oven to 300°F. Heat 2 tablespoons of the olive oil in a large skillet over medium-high heat. Working in batches, brown the chicken all over, about 5 minutes. Transfer the pieces to a plate as they are cooked, and set aside.

Add the remaining 1 tablespoon olive oil to the same skillet and reduce the heat to medium. Add the onions and cook, scraping up any browned bits and stirring often, until the onions are soft, about 5 minutes. Transfer the onions to a large tagine or ceramic baking dish. Add the chickpeas. Arrange the chicken over the onions and chickpeas. Scatter the preserved lemon and olives around the chicken. Tuck the cinnamon sticks between the chicken. Pour the broth into the tagine. Cover the tagine with the lid or the dish with aluminum foil. Bake the tagine until it is bubbling hot and the chicken is cooked through, about 1 hour.

9.

Pantry Staples & Preserved Specialties

Everything you need to craft your best dish

Keeping your kitchen stocked with essential Mediterranean ingredients is your guarantee that a healthy snack or delicious meal is never out of reach. Here are the go-to items that we reach for in our own pantry.

Pan-Starters

Whether you're sautéing, stir-frying, or making a sauce from scratch, using high-quality oil and aromatics are the first steps toward a great meal.

- Canola Oil
- Extra-Virgin Olive Oil
- Garlic
- Grapeseed Oil
- Shallots
- Stock (use in place of water)
- Tomatoes, Diced & Canned
- Tomato Paste
- Wine

Bright Finishes

Adding a touch of acidity is a chef's trick for finishing a well-balanced dish.

- Balsamic Vinegar, aged
- Cider Vinegar
- Lemon, fresh or preserved
- Red Wine
- Sherry Vinegar
- Verjus (red or white unfermented grape juice)
- White Wine

Herbs
& Spices

Fresh or dried herbs and
spices add zest and depth.

DRY

- Bay Leaves
- Coriander
- Cracked Black Pepper
- Cumin
- Herbes de Provence
- Oregano
- Red Pepper Flakes
- Sea Salt
- Smoked Paprika
- Thyme

FRESH

- Basil
- Cilantro
- Dill
- Mint
- Parsley
- Rosemary

Condiments
& Spreads

Tossed, topped, or spread, these
ingredients often turn a basic dish
into a Mediterranean masterpiece.

- Capers
- Cornichons
- Dijon Mustard
- Extra-Virgin Olive Oil
- Fruit Preserves (fig, sour cherry,
  lemon, etc.)
- Olive Spread
- Olives, pitted
- Roasted Peppers

Whole Grains, Beans & Nuts

A staple of the Mediterranean diet, beans and grains add protein and fiber to the foundation of a dish. Nuts, a go-to snack, are also a healthy option for adding crunch to salads.

- Almonds
- Arborio Rice
- Bulgur Wheat
- Chickpeas
- Couscous
- Lentils
- Pasta
- Quinoa
- Walnuts

Dairy

Healthy fats and lean proteins star in the Mediterranean diet.

- Eggs
- Feta
- Greek yogurt
- Goat cheese
- Parmigiano-Reggiano

Preserved Fish & Cured Meats

Often the star ingredient in a dish, these pantry favorites pack a lot of flavor.

- Anchovies
- Chorizo
- Pancetta
- Prosciutto
- Sardines
- Tuna packed in olive oil

TIP

Prosciutto, pancetta, and chorizo are typically a component of cheese boards and sandwiches, but they also render wonderful flavor when heated and crisped in a pan with olive oil, shallots, and garlic. Toss this mixture into wilted greens, grains, salads, and pasta.

Preserved & Pickled Specialties

The time-honored craft of pickling and preserving in-season vegetables is a cornerstone of Mediterranean snacking, entertaining, and cooking.

Years ago, many of these ingredients were only found in specialty cheese shops across metropolitan cities. More recently we have seen tremendous growth in demand and accessibility. Consumers are recognizing that preserved vegetables effectively lock in the season's best flavor.

Whether you are snacking, entertaining or cooking a family meal, incorporating these ingredients is one of the easiest ways to customize your dish, adding both nutrition and flavor. We hope you enjoy taking a closer look at some of our favorites.

Artichokes

According to Greek mythology, when Zeus grew bored of the women on Mount Olympus, he would visit Earth in hopes of attracting a new love. It was there that he became enchanted with a beauty named Cynara. Unfortunately, the feelings were not mutual and when Cynara turned Zeus down, he hurled a lightning bolt at her and turned her into an artichoke.

Thus the origin of the scientific name for an artichoke: *Cynara cardunculus*.

CLASSIC USE
In Italy it is quite common for long-stem artichokes to be served "Roman style:" sliced lengthwise and topped with fresh herbs, lemon, and shaved Parmigiano-Reggiano. Artichokes served this way may also be grilled or braised.

MODERN USE
Artichoke spread is a fun twist on the classic Italian pesto. Different combinations can go into a pesto, but typically you purée the artichokes with fresh herbs (basil, parsley), lemon, garlic, olive oil, and nuts (pine, walnut, almonds).

Beldi Olives (Dry/Oil Cured)

Moroccan olives are most famously sold in "souqs," the large markets in towns like Marrakesh and Fez. Market stalls line the streets with vast displays of olives, spices, preserved lemons, and other specialties stacked high, awaiting the daily rush of locals.

CLASSIC USE

Tagine, the name of both the cooking vessel and the signature meal of Morocco, is in fact an earlier version of what we today call a crockpot dinner. Tagines (the recipe) are made from different combinations of lamb, chicken, fish, vegetables, olives, fruits, seeds, and nuts. Tagines (the vessel) trap steam and push moisture back down into the stew.

MODERN USE

Beldi olives are deeply fruity and bold-flavored, meaning a little goes a long way. Puréeing them with olive oil, thyme, and garlic creates a vibrant spread that pairs delightfully with fresh orange segments and arugula. Spread it on crusty bread and appetizers are served!

Capers

Wondering about the difference between a caper and a caperberry? Simply put, the caper is the unopened bud of the caper plant. If left to grow into a flower, the caperberry will emerge as the fully matured fruit. Caper buds are classified by their size, ranging from nonpareil (up to 7mm) up to grusas (14+mm). While smaller capers may be easier to top and toss, larger sizes such as capotes (9-11mm) can pack an impressive amount of flavor.

CLASSIC USE
Puttanesca sauce is made with tomatoes, capers, anchovies, pitted black olives (Gaeta, if you can find them), garlic, and olive oil. It is generally served with pasta, but can also be spooned over chicken, seared tuna, and swordfish.

MODERN USE
Pan-fried capers are a delightfully floral treat that can be tossed over everything from roasted Brussels sprouts to a bagel with cream cheese and lox. For an extra bonus, keep the caper oil after frying and use it to dress greens, grains, or pasta.

Castelvetrano Olives

Are Castelvetrano naturally bright green? In short, yes. Native to the town of Castelvetrano (near Sicily in the Belice Valley), these olives are picked by hand, kept in refrigeration, and cured without fermentation. This locks in their vibrant color prior to being packaged.

CLASSIC USE
Often referred to as a "starter olive" due to its fresh, mild, and sweet flavor profile, Castelvetrano olives are the perfect choice to serve with cocktails at a large gathering. If martinis are on the menu, these gemlike olives are the perfect garnish.

MODERN USE
The mild sweetness of the Castelvetrano makes it a perfect addition to a cold pasta salad dressed with EVOO, lemon, capers, and garlic. Top it off with some fresh ricotta, Pecorino, or Parmigiano-Reggiano.

Cerignola

Bella di Cerignola translates to "the beautiful one from Cerignola" in Italian. Grown in Puglia, the heel of Italy's boot, these large and meaty olives are naturally found as green (mild and buttery) or black (fruity and nutty).

CLASSIC USE

Bella di Cerignola olives are an integral part of the traditional Italian antipasto course. If you find yourself in the Puglia region (lucky you!), be on the lookout for taralli, a fennel-infused cracker that is often served with olives instead of fresh bread.

MODERN USE

Because they're one of the larger and milder varietals of olives, Bella di Cerignola lend themselves to being infused with herbs, spices, and fruit. A beautiful mason jar of marinated olives can make a charming hostess gift over the holidays.

Cornichon

Smaller and crisper than the traditional dill pickles favored by Eastern Europeans and less sweet than most pickles found in the United States, cornichons require quick and sometimes multiple harvests per day to ensure that they remain petite (often around 2 inches).

CLASSIC USE
In France, cornichons are an integral part of several classic dishes:

Charcuterie Plates
A beautiful platter of thinly sliced prosciutto or ham, pâté, Dijon mustard, baguette, and a soft sheep's milk cheese.

Choucroute Garnie
A wintertime favorite in the Alsace region, cornichons often garnish this hearty platter of assorted meats, sauerkraut, and potatoes.

Tartare Sauce
A condiment often used to top fried or broiled fish, a classic French tartare sauce is made with cornichons, mayonnaise, Dijon mustards, capers, lemon, and tarragon.

MODERN USE
Cornichons add the perfect amount of brightness and tang to tuna, egg, and chicken salad sandwiches.

Dolmas
(Stuffed Grape Leaves)

Dolmas are a centerpiece of both Greek and Turkish cuisine. If your family is from either country, chances are good that your grandmother has the "best" recipe. Also known as dolmades or stuffed grape leaves, the word "dolma" dates back to the Ottoman Empire and loosely translates into "to be stuffed." Each culture takes great pride in their regional recipes, which include both savory and sweet variations:

CLASSIC USE

In Greece, dolmas are typically stuffed with seasoned ground lamb, creamy rice, dill, mint, lemon, onion, and pine nuts. Often served warm, they may be braised in a traditional avgolemono (lemon and egg) sauce or served with a side of tzatziki (yogurt and cucumber).

Turkey has a similar recipe for meat and rice filled dolmas that they often braise in a light tomato sauce. Beyond that, they also favor a sweeter dolma that is filled with creamy rice, pine nuts, currants, mint, allspice, cinnamon, and a touch of sugar.

Both cultures serve dolmas warm or at room temperature as part of the meze or appetizer course.

MODERN USE

For a savory approach, try wrapping dolmas with prosciutto. Serve with some freshly sliced cantaloupe to sweeten the mood.

Extra-Virgin Olive Oil

Selecting the right extra-virgin olive oil can seem daunting. Like wine, there are countless different regions, styles, and flavor profiles. "What is good?" is a question of personal preference. Flavor profiles often vary by the region in which they are produced. For example, an EVOO from southern Spain is typically pungent and bold compared to the sweeter, more delicate oil that comes from Puglia, Italy. Trying different styles is the best way to uncover your personal favorite.

Unlike wine, extra-virgin olive oil does not improve with age. The time between harvest to crush, crush to bottle, and bottle to table is critical for flavor and quality. Storage is also vital to keeping EVOO fresh. Ideally, oil should be stored in a dark, airtight container in a cool temperature.

CLASSIC USE
The gold standard of the Mediterranean diet, extra-virgin olive oil has been used for millennia as a sauté, dressing, marinade, and dipping oil. A good rule of thumb: when you'd use butter, you can use extra-virgin olive oil.

MODERN USE
In recent years, extra-virgin olive oil has become a popular dessert ingredient. Buttery, sweet, and herbal, olive oil gelato typifies one of our favorite aspects of the Med diet: it is okay to indulge if you do it with high-quality, natural ingredients.

Fig Preserves

Like olives, figs have been a symbol of prosperity and peace since biblical times. Figs in fifth-century B.C. Athens were valued so highly that exporting them was illegal.

CLASSIC USE

Fig preserves have long been a staple of cheese and antipasto platters across the Mediterranean. The deep, rich sweetness of the fig and notes of honey and caramel uniquely qualify it to pair with almost any cheese.

MODERN USE

Fig spread is a decadent base for a desert tart or sweet and savory pizza. In fact, the same items that are often paired with fig spread on cheese boards (prosciutto, goat cheese, blue cheese) make the perfect pizza toppings.

Fleur de Sel (Sea Salt)

To harvest sea salt, ocean water is flowed into marshes and the salt from the water eventually rises to the surface in thin layers. One of the most prized types of sea salt is fleur de sel, a French salt known for its high moisture content and uniquely flaky texture that doesn't immediately dissolve over hot food. This makes fleur de sel an ideal finishing salt.

CLASSIC USE
Sole Meunière, credited as the dish that inspired Julia Child on her culinary path, is a classic French dish that is simply a lightly floured fillet of sole, pan-fried in clarified butter and topped with fresh herbs, lemon, and fleur de sel.

MODERN USE
Fleur de sel has become a popular ingredient for pastry chefs as they craft deserts that satisfy both the sweet and salty craving. Fleur de sel is routinely used in salted caramel, sprinkled over chocolate ice cream (sometimes with olive oil), or even added to the top of pastries like scones and muffins.

French Olives: Lucque, Picholine & Niçoise Olives

Lucques, Picholine and Niçoise are considered to be among the most prized table olives. Lucques, the gem of Provence, are lovingly referred to by locals as "green diamonds." Picholine, sometimes called "fausse Lucques" (false Lucques) in jest are more formally named "Picholine de Languedoc" after their native growing region. "Cailletier" is the varietal name of the authentic Niçoise olive from Nice.

CLASSIC USE
Classic French table olives are typically served with a soft sheep's milk cheese, bread, charcuterie, and pâté.

MODERN USE
Champagne and olives is not necessarily a typical pairing but the crispness and saltiness of certain French varietals like the Lucque and Picholine actually balance nicely with the sweetness of champagne.

Gigandes Beans

Gigandes (Greek for "giant") can also be called Gigantes (pronounced YEE-gahn-tess) or elephant beans. They are prized throughout Greece for being plump and firm, yet creamy and buttery.

CLASSIC USE
Gigandes beans marinated in tomato sauce is Greek comfort food at its finest. A traditional baked Gigandes bean and tomato casserole includes fresh oregano and dill and is typically served warm (sometimes with Feta).

MODERN USE
It's quick and simple to make homemade hummus by pureeing Gigandes beans with olive oil, lemon, and garlic. This spread is great on sandwiches and wraps, as well as for dipping veggies.

Halkidiki Olives (Mt. Athos)

The peninsula of Halkidiki is dotted with centuries-old Greek Orthodox monasteries. One-third of the peninsula is occupied by Mount Athos, a famous tenth-century monastery. These hills, descending to the Aegean Sea, are the ideal terroir for growing olives. Halkidiki's are large in size and mild in flavor, making them ideal for stuffing.

CLASSIC USE
The standard-bearer of Greek green olives, Halkidiki's (also known as Mount Athos olives) have traditionally been the star ingredient in fresh chopped salads or served with feta cheese, hummus, and pita.

MODERN USE
Stuff a Halkidiki olive with feta, cheddar, or mozzarella cheese, wrap it in puff pastry dough, and bake. (And make a second batch, you'll need it!)

Kalamata Olives

Have you ever heard of a Black Crow olive? Legend has it that some Spartans use this name for the Kalamata as an homage to its beaklike shape and dark color.

CLASSIC USE
It is hard to find a more classic use for Kalamata olives than in a traditional Greek salad. Its briny, smoky, and fruity taste is the perfect complement to feta, cucumber, onion, tomato, and field greens.

MODERN USE
Kalamata olives are an interesting choice for marinated and roasting. They combine well with many spices, herbs, and fresh ingredients that enhance the flavor of the olives. Try herbs like lavender, basil, oregano, and thyme or fresh citrus zest from oranges and lemons.

Marinated Beets

Has anyone ever described your face as being "red as a beet?" Perhaps they're familiar with an old custom: during the nineteenth century, women used beet juice as a cheek stain or lipstick.

CLASSIC USE
Across the Mediterranean, beets are a prevalent and inexpensive ingredient that is often served as a component in salad and side dishes. In Turkey, for example, marinated and roasted beets in yogurt sauce is favorite of the locals.

MODERN USE
An heirloom tomato salad with marinated beets, feta cheese, and fresh herbs (cilantro or basil) captures the fresh flavors of summer, pure and simple.

Marinated Mushrooms

Mushroom growing made its way to America in the late 1800s. The early success stories of mushroom harvesting came from florists, who could place mushroom beds under their existing flower benches, thus creating an opportunity to double profits.

CLASSIC USE
Marinated mushrooms are a staple of the Italian-American antipasto platter, often combined with garlic, vinegar, oil, and spices. These plump and juicy gems are tossed into salads and pasta or served with cheese, charcuterie, and pickled vegetable platters.

MODERN USE
Marinated mushrooms are a great ingredient to toss into all types of pasta and rice dishes. From Italian risotto and lasagne all the way to an Asian-inspired stir-fry, mushrooms will add a nice earthiness and heartiness.

Roasted Tomatoes

Expect to use 4 to 5 pounds of fresh tomatoes to make one pound of roasted tomatoes. Contrary to most advice and recipes, the "slow and low" technique will provide you with the sweetest and most robust-tasting roasted tomato.

CLASSIC USE
The simple and always popular Caprese salad is a year-round hit when you use roasted tomatoes with fresh mozzarella, fresh basil, and a drizzle of aged balsamic vinegar.

MODERN USE
Roasted tomatoes for breakfast? The juicy, sweet, and robust tomatoes are heaven on whole grain toast with a soft-boiled egg.

Preserved Lemons

Sometimes called "country lemons," preserved lemons were originally created as a way to enjoy the popular summer fruit year-round. Traditionally used in Moroccan and North African cuisine, it's the peel (not the juice) of a preserved lemon that is often used in recipes.

CLASSIC USE
Skillet chicken with preserved lemons and green olives is a classic Moroccan dish that is chock-full of aromatics, herbs, and spices such as ginger, coriander, saffron, garlic, and onion.

MODERN USE
Adding some zest from the rind of a preserved lemon is a nice way to brighten up the classic holiday sugar cookie.

Roasted Peppers

Every August, the town of Aetos in Greece gathers for the "Feast of the Pepper." The festival is marked by dancing, music, and feasting on a range of pepper dishes cooked by the locals. In this town, as in many across Greece and Turkey, the pepper is considered part of what nurtures community, commerce, and heritage.

CLASSIC USE
Roasted peppers are a mainstay of the traditional Greek meze plate, typically paired with hummus, pita, olives, stuffed grape leaves, and feta cheese.

MODERN USE
Roasted peppers are a wonderful way to add a touch of sweetness and smokiness to any dish. Create a vibrant sauce for grilled meats by rough-chopping roasted peppers and mixing them with garlic, olive oil, and fresh herbs like cilantro or basil.

Tapenade

Tapenade takes its names from *tapeno*, the Provençal word for "caper." In fact, early tapenade recipes from the region were typically made from equal parts capers, olives, and fish (either anchovies or tuna). In later years, especially in countries like Greece and Italy, the olive became a more dominant ingredient.

CLASSIC USE
Across much of the Mediterranean, serving olive tapenade before a meal with toasted bread is as typical as serving bread with butter in the United States. Tapenade is also a classic topping for grilled chicken and fish.

MODERN USE
Make your tuna salad Mediterranean by mixing in a small amount of olive tapenade and a drizzle of EVOO in place of mayonnaise. This twist on a sandwich classic is also great stuffed inside an avocado.

Stuffed Olives

Stuffing olives can be a fun way to get kids involved in making healthy choices and learning about Mediterranean diet ingredients. Take some pitted olives and an array of stuffing selections (cheese, sundried tomatoes, almonds, garlic, peppers, etc.) and let everyone create their own stuffed olives.

CLASSIC USE
Stuffed olives are considered classic garnishes in cocktails such as the martini and Bloody Mary. Of course, a dirty martini takes it a step further by adding olive brine to the drink.

MODERN USE
Fried and stuffed olives are starting to pop up everywhere these days! A modern take on favorite appetizers like mozzarella sticks and jalapeño poppers, fried and stuffed olives are an irresistible one-bite appetizer.

Acknowledgments

We are both inspired and humbled by the company we get to keep. Thank you for sharing in our journey and cheers to what is still to come!

To the FOODMatch team: for the knowledge, dedication, and innovation that is consistently displayed to service our customers and community. Every single one of you plays such an integral role in our shared success. Take a moment to appreciate all we've created together.

To our partners across the world in the fields, on the production lines, and working to help us secure the finest products available: your job is tireless and your effort exceptional. Thank you for continuing the time-honored culinary traditions that define your heritage that can now help shape a new generation of food lovers.

To our grocery and foodservice partners who have helped build and solidify the Mediterranean category with consumers across the United States, we value your unwavering commitment to quality. Thank you for your loyalty and support.

To Melissa Hamilton and Christopher Hirsheimer: you have been our beacon, creatively guiding us through the process of uncovering what this project looked like, why it was important, and how it could be used. Your spirit and influence can be seen on every page, in every recipe. You took a simple idea sparked at a cocktail party and transformed it into something substantive and remarkable.

To Valerie Saint-Rossy, our copy editor, who always seems to know what we mean to say and how to say it better.

Mediterranean Diet Resources

OLDWAYS

Inspiring good health through the preservation of heritage diets and cultural food traditions, Oldways pioneered the Mediterranean Diet Pyramid in 1993. After more than 25 years, Oldways work continues across a broad base of programming, including the Whole Grains Council, Mediterranean Food Alliance, Nutrition Exchange, and Cheese Coalition.

info@oldwayspt.org

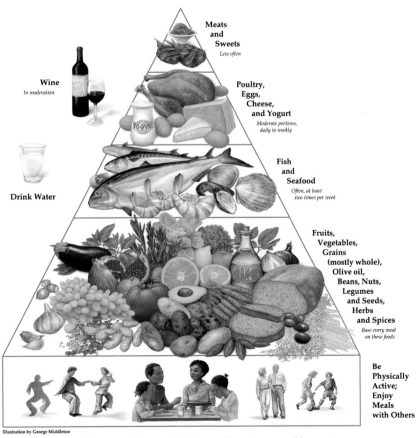

Measurement Conversions

US DRY VOLUME MEASUREMENTS

¹⁄₁₆ teaspoon	dash
⅛ teaspoon	a pinch
3 teaspoons	1 Tablespoon
⅛ cup	2 tablespoons
¼ cup	4 Tablespoons
⅓ cup	5 Tablespoons plus 1 teaspoon
½ cup	8 Tablespoons
¾ cup	12 Tablespoons
1 cup	16 Tablespoons
1 Pound	16 ounces

US LIQUID VOLUME MEASUREMENTS

8 Fluid ounces	1 Cup
1 Pint	2 Cups
1 Quart	2 Pints
1 Gallon	4 Quarts

US TO METRIC CONVERSIONS

⅕ teaspoon	1 ml
1 teaspoon	5 ml
1 tablespoon	15 ml
1 fluid oz.	30 ml
⅕ cup	50 ml
1 cup	240 ml
2 cups (1 pint)	470 ml
4 cups (1 quart)	.95 liter
4 quarts (1 gal.)	3.8 liters
1 oz.	28 grams
1 pound	454 grams

OVEN TEMPERATURE CONVERSIONS

FAHRENHEIT	CELSIUS
275º F	140º C
300º F	150º C
325º F	165º C
350º F	180º C
375º F	190º C
400º F	200º C
425º F	220º C
450º F	230º C
475º F	240º C

Index

A

In 1999, during a trip to Crete, Phil Meldrum plants an olive tree.